The Q Guide to

Soap Operas

The Q Guides

FROM ALYSON BOOKS

POP CULTURE

Q

OUT THERE

GUIDE

The Q Guide to

Soap Operas

**Stuff You Didn't Even Know You
Wanted to Know . . .** about divas, hunks,
and the best-kept closets in daytime

[daniel r. coleridge]

© 2006 BY DANIEL R. COLERIDGE

MANUFACTURED IN THE UNITED STATES OF AMERICA.

THIS TRADE PAPERBACK ORIGINAL IS PUBLISHED BY
ALYSON BOOKS
P.O. BOX 1253,
OLD CHELSEA STATION,
NEW YORK, NEW YORK 10113-1251

DISTRIBUTION IN THE UNITED KINGDOM BY
TURNAROUND PUBLISHER SERVICES
UNIT 3, OLYMPIA TRADING ESTATE
COBURG ROAD, WOOD GREEN
LONDON 722 6TZ ENGLAND.

FIRST EDITION: SEPTEMBER 2006

06 07 08 09 10 **a** 10 9 8 7 6 5 4 3 2 1

ISBN-10 1-55583-986-X
ISBN-13 978-1-55583-985-4

LIBRARY OF CONGRESS
CATALOGING-IN-PUBLICATION DATA IS ON FILE.

For my mother, Maria

Contents

THE AUTHOR OF *THE Q GUIDE TO SOAP OPERAS* ON
SET AT ABC'S *GENERAL HOSPITAL*, ALONGSIDE BEN
HOGESTYN AS "LUCAS JONES," AND ANTHONY GEARY,
AS "LUKE SPENCER." (© SCOTT GARFIELD/AMERICAN
BROADCASTING COMPANIES, INC.)

Introduction

QUOTE

"Ever notice how dead soap characters always have perfect-looking head shots?"

MY NAME is Daniel and I'm a soap-opera addict. Since age eleven, I have been obsessed with watching sex and suffering in the afternoon. Actually, it might have begun earlier than that.

"I was pregnant with you during the summer of '74," my mother recalls. "I couldn't go out into the sun and the heat because I would faint, so I stayed inside the house with the air conditioning. I would only come out in the dark of night, like a vampire. During the day, what else did I have to do but watch soap operas? I would get *so* caught up, that I sat there screaming at the television set! Just when I was close to giving birth to you, I was watching *One Life to Live*. Tommy Lee Jones was playing a doctor and somebody else was doing something dirty to Viki Lord's sister, Meredith. It got to the point where I was getting so mad at the TV that I threw a coffee cup at it. The cup missed the TV and smashed up against the wall in a million pieces. Once I did that, I said, 'Ya know, this is getting a little too intense. Now it's time to quit watching soap operas.' But it was too late. It infected the baby. My baby became a soap-opera queen in utero!"

Scary as it sounds, I think Mommy is right! Ultimately I grew up to write a soap column for TVGuide.com that reaches millions of my fellow daytime TV devotees. That's how I got invited to check into ABC's *General Hospital* recently to be an extra at the funeral of Dr. Tony Jones. This gay boy was the happiest mourner you've ever seen!

Poor Tony perished in a viral epidemic that struck the fictional town of Port Charles, just in time for February sweeps. The writers killed off Courtney Jacks, played by Alicia Leigh Willis, a popular blonde who opted not to renew her contract because she was itching to pursue roles in primetime series and films. They also nixed Tony's talented portrayer, Brad Maule, a cast member since 1984, who hadn't had much to do on *GH* in recent years. So there I was on the soap's Hollywood set, seated in a pew in the famous hospital chapel, helping my favorite daytime actors say good-bye to one of their freshly unemployed costars. That's showbiz.

Still, for an acting rookie like me, it was all a bit surreal. Fortunately, I was not required to cry on cue or call undue attention to myself. I merely had to dress in my black Prada suit, slick back my hair and look solemn, while the legendary Anthony Geary—that's Luke Spencer of "Luke and Laura" fame—delivered a touching eulogy. Between takes, the cast chitchatted to break up a long day of shooting. Geary told us a bawdy "frog and the rabbi" joke he borrowed from Robin Williams. Aussie actor Tristan Rogers—aka supercop Robert Scorpio—told me about his fave Tex-Mex takeout place in Los Angeles. And Jane Elliot, who plays the wicked and witty Tracy Quartermaine, pointed to Brad Maule's handsome photograph on the altar. "Ever notice how dead soap characters always have perfect-looking head shots on display at these memorials?" she said with a wink. "Maybe Tony was a realtor on the side."

Later, I was all ears, as some actors gossiped about a well-known *GH* star—now acting on another popular sudser—whom they consider "a horrible human being." Sorry, I can't name names! Even so, I couldn't help but wonder how a nice queer kid like me came to be sitting here, dishing with these soap stars like an old pro. Well, I started out as a homo at home, watching them on TV, just like you!

There are devoted legions of us gay and lesbian soap fans out there because, like Luke and Laura, we've suffered heartache and we like a little romantic escapism to distract us. Especially if it involves hunky men, fabulous clothes, and lots of sassy one-liners! Aside from sex-drenched, over-the-top madness, we're also attached to the close-knit core families, around which all soap worlds turn. Gays often grow up feeling different and isolated, so it's a comfort to watch rule-breakers being loved no matter what—even if they are boyfriend-stealing baby-switchers with multiple personalities.

The Q Guide to Soap Operas explores everything

gay about the daytime soaps. You'll learn more about why so many of us GLBT viewers can't resist tuning in to supposedly "straight" TV serials. We'll dish our favorite hunks and divas, as well as all the gay and lesbian characters which have made queer appearances over the years. We'll also peek behind the closet door of daytime drama, for a glimpse of the bent actors who've made their glorious careers playing it straight in the suds. For the *Young and Restless* overachievers among you, there'll be bitch-slapping quizzes to test your soap knowledge.

So pour yourself a glass of champers, break out the Godiva bonbons, and tell Winifred the maid to hold all your calls, honey. We only have *One Life to Live* and there's a big *Bold and Beautiful* world of soaps to cover. Fortunately, this book is your gay *Guiding Light* to all of it. OK, was that last quip *too* queer? I know. Just read on . . . *All My Children* will appreciate my punny sense of humor in time.

—DANIEL R. COLERIDGE,
FEBRUARY 2006

The Q Guide to
Soap Operas

LONGTIME GENOA CITY RESIDENT KATHERINE
CHANCELLOR IS PLAYED BY THE LEGENDARY JEANNE
COOPER ON CBS'S *THE YOUNG AND THE RESTLESS.*
(COURTESY OF CHARLES BUSH)

CHAPTER ONE

Soap History 101

> "We burst out in 1973 in daytime TV."

LISTEN UP, soap-opera fanatics. It's time you were schooled on your sudsy roots.

Long before the soaps sizzled on afternoon TV, they started out as fifteen-minute radio serials. Starting in the 1930s, an avid audience of 40 million American housewives got their daily dose of melodrama by listening to shows like *Ma Perkins, The Romance of Helen Trent* and *Young Dr. Malone.* These daytime dramas were dubbed "soap operas" because their sponsors advertised soap and sundry other products to a captive audience of bored homemakers. They also made for a pleasant diversion from the harsh realities of everyday life during the Great Depression. As we all know, it's depressing to be poor!

The age of radio serials lasted about a quarter of a century, until TV overtook radio around the mid-1950s. TV's longest-running sudser is CBS's seventy-year-old *Guiding Light*, which started out as a radio serial way back in 1937! In the 1950s and early '60s, the soaps were not yet ready for bare-chested hunks and steamy bedroom scenes. Soap characters kept their clothes on and chattered in kitchens and hospital wards. They remained mostly indoors, due to the production limitations of the time.

"It was very simple," recalls Helen Wagner, 88, who has played Nancy Hughes on *As the World Turns* since the show's pilot episode aired on April 2, 1956. "Nancy was a homebody. I did everything around the house. I served coffee, fixed a meal, washed the dishes and all the things that a woman does during the day. We couldn't move from set to set, so characters mostly came in and out of the kitchen. When we began to do the show on tape, we could make trips out elsewhere."

Soaps were spiced up in the mid-60s with riskier plots about adultery, rape and "Who's your daddy?" paternity enigmas. The '70s brought more focus on young lovers, and sex on the screen in general. "We burst out in 1973 in daytime TV," says Jeanne Cooper of *The Young and the Restless*, which gave us teenagers traipsing around in skimpy Speedos and bikinis, sudsy shower sex, and the first STD case on the soaps!

The '80s are considered the golden age of soap operas. Daytime ratings were hot, storylines were full of sex, science fiction, and high adventure, and there were big budgets for location shoots in far-flung places. The term *supercouple* was coined to describe popular pairings like *General Hospital's* Luke and Laura, *Days of our Lives's* Bo and Hope, and *Santa Barbara's* Cruz and Eden. Nighttime soaps like *Dallas, Dynasty, Falcon Crest,* and *Knots Landing* were also highly successful.

The soaps began to struggle in the '90s due to changes in the times. Cable and satellite television offered viewers more channels and choices than

Soap History

1. Who made soap history by contracting daytime's first STD (sexually transmitted disease) in 1978?

    a. *Erica Kane,* All My Children
    b. *Nikki Reed,* The Young and the Restless
    c. *Laura Vining,* General Hospital
    d. *Barbara Ryan,* As the World Turns

2. In what year was the Daytime Emmy Awards ceremony first broadcast on primetime TV?

    a. *1974*
    b. *1980*
    c. *1991*
    d. *1992*

3. Which of these classic afternoon soaps of yesteryear ran the longest?

    a. Search for Tomorrow
    b. The Secret Storm
    c. Love of Life
    d. The Edge of Night

Soap History

4. Who is the legendary writer credited with creating the very first soap opera?

   a. William J. Bell, Sr.
   b. Douglas Marland
   c. Agnes Nixon
   d. Irna Phillips

5. Which of these soaps was not a spin-off of *Another World*?

   a. Texas
   b. Somerset
   c. As the World Turns

ever before. The coveted advertising demographic of females age eighteen to forty-nine proved increasingly elusive, as more and more women worked outside the home. In 1995, the afternoon soaps were pre-empted by constant news coverage of O. J. Simpson's lengthy murder trial. This real-life melodrama seriously hurt the continuity of stories and broke many longtime soap viewers' tune-in habits. One historic low point occurred when NBC axed *Another World* in 1999, after thirty-five years on the air. The Peacock network also launched the late Aaron Spelling's *Sunset Beach* in 1997, only to cancel it within two years due to disappointing ratings.

In the twenty-first century, budgetary belts are being tightened and cancellation rumors haunt a few other shows. Nevertheless, there are still millions of us soap-opera addicts out there watching, obsessing over, and supporting our sudsers everyday! Daytime execs are also seeking innovative ways to lure in new and lapsed viewers. The fabulous cable channel SOAPnet currently broadcasts five of the nine daytime soaps at night. Soaps are podcasting episodes. They're also bringing back popular characters from the '80s (*Days of our Lives*'s Patch and Kayla, *General Hospital*'s Robert, Holly, and Anna) in hopes of wooing back nostalgic fans.

NO SOAP IS COMPLETE WITHOUT A RESIDENT HOTTIE, AND CBS'S *THE YOUNG AND THE RESTLESS* HAS ONE IN "NICHOLAS NEWMAN," AS PLAYED BY JOSHUA MORROW. (COURTESY OF CBS-TV)

CHAPTER TWO

Know Your Daytime Soaps

QUOTE

"I would naturally love to see her come back."

THERE ARE currently nine daytime soap operas on the air. That's nine hours of sudsy drama a day, five days a week, fifty-two weeks a year! And since the average soap's cast boasts thirty to forty actors—who work either on contract or recurring status—there are —*lots* of sordid lives to keep track of. Here's a queer's quickie rundown of each show's vital stats, plus a few suggestions for the best current stuff to sample if you tune in tomorrow!

All My Children

DEBUT: January 5, 1970, on ABC
SETTING: Pine Valley, Pennsylvania
HERE'S THE SITCH: Created by Agnes Nixon, the splashy sudser has always centered around Erica Kane, the über-sexy maneater played by Susan Lucci. Thanks to *AMC*'s fertility-obsessed head writer Megan McTavish, many of today's twisted tales concern

Children with fascinatingly unusual origins. FYI, Erica had TV's first legal abortion in 1973, soon after the U.S. Supreme Court's historic *Roe v. Wade* decision. In a controversial stroke of revisionist history, *AMC* resurrected Erica's child in 2006, with an outré plot about a mad gynecologist who somehow stole her fetus instead of terminating her pregnancy. Science and common sense be damned! Erica's "unaborted" son, Joshua Madden, is now an arrogant doctor played by sexy, strutting ex-model Colin Egglesfield. Alrighty then.

SIGNATURE SUPERCOUPLE: Dixie and Tad Martin (Cady McClain, Michael E. Knight)

TOWN SAINT: Bianca Montgomery (Eden Riegel). Erica Kane's out, proud, brave, and caring lesbian daughter has been victimized and all but canonized.

TOWN SLUT: Babe Carey Chandler (Alexa Havins). The trailer tart's many bedmates include hottie stepbrothers JR Chandler (Jacob Young) and Dr. Jamie Martin (Justin Bruening). Soap sluts have all the fun!

TOWN STUD: Ryan Lavery (Cameron Mathison). Read more about him in the Top 10 Soap Hunks chapter.

TOWN PSYCHO: Janet "From Another Planet" Dillon. Both Kate Collins and Robin Mattson have played Pine Valley's campiest cuckoo, who famously threw her sister, Natalie, down a well and stole her identity in 1991. Janet *still* moans and complains about her prettier sis getting favoritism, even though Nat died in a car crash years ago. Get over it already!

As the World Turns

DEBUT: April 2, 1956, on CBS

SETTING: Oakdale, Illinois

HERE'S THE SITCH: Created by Irna Phillips, the venerable fifty-year-old soap follows the lives of the Hughes, Ryan, Snyder, and Walsh clans. *World Turns* is one of daytime's champs at weaving social issues into soapy storytelling, while keeping it entertaining. The coming out story of Luke Snyder (Van Hansis) has been realistically and sensitively told. Every member of his family gets into the action! Elsewhere in Oakdale, Barbie doll Katie Peretti (Terri Colombino) gets all the hottest boyfriends, while other Oakdale women harbor dysfunctional desires for that two-faced, chronic liar Paul Ryan (Roger Howarth). *Ugh!* Paul makes us *so* mad. It's a mystery how Mr. Bottle Blond finds the time to get those highlights done on his long tresses, when he's constantly busy deceiving everyone.

SIGNATURE SUPERCOUPLE: Lily and Holden Snyder (Martha Byrne, Jon Hensley). Conceived by the show's late, great head writer, Douglas Marland, the continuing love story of rich girl Lily, and her former stable boy Holden, is timeless.

TOWN SAINT: Gwen Norbeck Munson (Jennifer Landon). Despite tough breaks—including empty pockets and a boozy, floozy mother—Gwen is a likable everywoman who works hard, stays honest, and keeps it real. (Extra saintly points go to Ms.

Landon for being the daughter of the late *Highway to Heaven* star Michael Landon!)

TOWN SLUT: Carly Tenney Snyder (Maura West). She seduced her rich sister's man and then *tried* to reform her ways, but this desperate housewife always slips back into Slutsville. Case in point: Carly's recent gig as a go-go dancer at the shady Galaxy strip club.

TOWN STUD: Mike Kasnoff (Mark Collier). Read more about him in the Top 10 Soap Hunks chapter.

TOWN PSYCHO: Emily Stewart (Kelly Menighan Hensley). Beware of an insecure, clingy woman with a gun. "Paul, I love you-*hoo-hoo!*"

The Bold and the Beautiful

DEBUT: March 23, 1987, on CBS

SETTING: Los Angeles, California

HERE'S THE SITCH: Created by Lee Phillip and William J. Bell, this is the sister soap of *The Young and the Restless*. It was originally entitled *Rags* and set in the Bells' hometown of Chicago, Illinois, in preproduction. But by the time *B&B* made it to air, the setting was L.A., where the soap is actually taped. In the sun-drenched world of Southern California fashion, the haughty Forrester family reigns supreme-and they sure know it. Machiavellian matriarch Stephanie Douglas Forrester (Susan Flannery) has fought an endless feud with her beautiful younger rival, Brooke Logan (Katherine Kelly Lang), "the slut from the Valley" who seduced Steph's husband Eric (John McCook) and *both* of her sons, Ridge

(Ronn Moss) and Thorne (Winsor Harmon). After nearly twenty years, *B&B*'s head writer, Bradley Bell, still keeps his winning formula fresh, funny, and sexy.

SIGNATURE SUPERCOUPLE: Brooke Logan and Ridge Forrester. It's their "destiny" to be together, even if she has humped most of his male relatives—including, most recently, his long-lost half-brother Dominick Marone (Jack Wagner).

TOWN SAINT: It's a tie! There's Dr. Taylor Hayes Forrester (Hunter Tylo), a heroic psychiatrist who keeps losing Ridge to Brooke, despite returning from the dead, twice, to reunite with him. Fans couldn't blame Taylor when she eventually turned to drinking (especially because this lady's drug of choice is Chardonnay; red wine would leave unsightly stains on Taylor's lovely lips). *B&B*'s other candidate for sainthood is Brooke's loyal daughter, Dr. Bridget Forrester (Ashley Jones), who still loves Mom even after Brooke stole two of her husbands!

TOWN SLUT: Brooke Logan. The shameless wanton—who turned the Forrester family into an incestuous passion pit—has her own lingerie line called "Brooke's Bedroom." Enough said.

TOWN STUD: Ridge Forrester. His portrayer, former *Player* lead singer Ronn Moss, continues to leave fans crying "Baby Come Back" at his public appearances.

TOWN PSYCHO: Sheila Carter (Kimberlin Brown). Read more about her under *The Young and the Restless*.

Days of our Lives

DEBUT: November 8, 1965, on NBC

SETTING: Salem, USA

HERE'S THE SITCH: Created by Ted Corday, Irna Phillips, and Allan Chase, the Peacock network's most successful soap continues to be produced by Ted's son, Ken Corday. The show's signature is its famous hourglass logo and the epitaph: "Like sands through the hourglass, so are the days of our lives." The best-known *Days* heroine is still Dr. Marlena Evans (Deidre Hall), a beautiful, blonde psychiatrist who just may be the most frequently kidnapped woman in daytime soap-opera history. Many front-burner tales have revolved around "Doc": most memorably, Hall's real-life twin, Andrea Hall, played Marlena's devious twin sister, Samantha, as well as an oddball named Hattie Adams, who had plastic surgery to look like the sexy shrink. Many non-*Days* fans got hooked in 1995 because of Marlena's sinfully campy, demonic possession story, which was inspired by the 1973 horror classic *The Exorcist*. Several '80s supercouples remain popular on today's *Days*, especially Hope and Bo Brady (Kristian Alfonso, Peter Reckell), Jennifer and Jack Devereaux (Melissa Reeves, Matthew Ashford), and Kayla and Steve "Patch" Johnson (Mary Beth Evans, Stephen Nichols). Among the show's younger set, Marlena's scheming bitch of a daughter, Sami Brady (Alison Sweeney), is Salem's busiest blackmailer.

14

SIGNATURE SUPERCOUPLE: It's a tie! Dr. Marlena Evans and John Black (Drake Hogestyn) share the honors with Bo and Hope Brady.

TOWN SAINT Alice Horton. Frances Reid has appeared on *Days* since day one as Alice, the beloved Horton family matriarch and the idyllic grandmother many viewers at home wished they had in their lives.

TOWN SLUT: Kate Roberts. As played by the elegant, ageless Lauren Koslow, Kate is both a former call girl and the ex-mistress of Salem's most infamous villain, Stefano DiMera (Joseph Mascolo). She has also produced six children by four different fathers (though you'd never know it to look at the tricky bitch's slinky, svelte figure). Viva Kate!

TOWN STUD: Austin Reed (Austin Peck). Read more about the sex symbol also known as "Austin Pecs" in the Top 10 Soap Hunks chapter.

TOWN PSYCHO: Vivian Alamain. None of Salem's cavalcade of crackpots compare to Vivian, as played by the divine daytime veteran Louise Sorel. During her hilarious reign of terror, the witty, wicked Vivian, buried Dr. Carly Manning alive and tormented her from above ground via walkie-talkie. She also underwent in vitro fertilization to get pregnant with an embryo stolen from longtime rival Kate Roberts and her billionaire husband, Victor Kiriakis (John Aniston). The long list of Madame Alamain's sins goes on, but fans wish it were even longer. Bring back Viv! We miss her mischief terribly.

General Hospital

DEBUT: April 1, 1963, on ABC

SETTING: Port Charles, New York

HERE'S THE SITCH: Created by Doris and Frank Hursley, the highest-rated ABC soap currently splits its time between the doctors and nurses in the hospital and the Mafia dons shooting up the streets of Port Charles. Maurice Benard, and Steve Burton—who play emotionally troubled mobsters Michael "Sonny" Corinthos and Jason Morgan—are frequently on the front burner as *GH*'s resident heartthrob anti-heroes. Recently, the show also started a trend of bringing back popular characters from the 1980s and '90s, like Jane Elliot as rich bitch Tracy Quartermaine, Finola Hughes and Tristan Rogers as superspies Anna Devane and Robert Scorpio, Kimberly McCullough as their HIV-positive daughter Dr. Robin Scorpio, and Emma Samms as con artist Holly Sutton. Longtime *GH* icon Anthony Geary, who plays Luke Spencer, still sizzles mischievously on the front burner. Sadly, there's a perpetual hole in the show due to the absence of Genie Francis, who quit in 2002. Years later, Geary has only kind things to say about Laura and Genie Francis. "Luke can never move on from Laura," Geary points out. "He does what he can to survive, but Genie and I have been hyphenated as the characters 'Luke and Laura' from the beginning. I would naturally love to see her come back. It's between her and the powers that be, and I'm not in that circle. But I'd enjoy it, especially these days when we're recapturing some of the old A-group from the glory days. It would be nice to have her as well." Fortunately, Francis was scheduled to return to *GH* for a brief stint in October 2006.

SIGNATURE SUPERCOUPLE: Luke and Laura Spencer. No *GH* couple will *ever* come close to Luke and Laura at the zenith of their popularity.

TOWN SAINT: Elizabeth Webber (Rebecca Herbst). Luke's doll of a daughter-in-law raises her kids, covers the famed General Hospital nurses' station, and bounces back from every tragedy with a brave smile.

TOWN SLUT: Carly Corinthos. The mouthy vixen—currently played by Laura Wright—is the long-lost daughter of *GH*'s beloved Bobbie Spencer (Jackie Zeman), who left prostitution for a nursing career. Carly came to Port Charles and seduced Bobbie's husband to punish Mom for giving her up for adoption. We've lost count of all the mobsters and millionaires Carly's bedded ever since.

TOWN STUD: Prince Nikolas Cassadine (Tyler Christopher). Read more about him in the Top 10 Soap Hunks chapter.

TOWN PSYCHO: Manny Ruiz. (R.I.P) As played by the heavily tattooed and very scary character actor Robert LaSardo, Manny kidnapped, raped, and murdered his way into viewers' hearts. Kudos to the maniacal mobster for single-handedly causing the great train wreck of 2005!

Guiding Light

DEBUT: June 30, 1952, on CBS

SETTING: Springfield, USA

HERE'S THE SITCH: Created by Irna Phillips in 1937, the radio soap moved over to television in 1952. Originally titled *The Guiding Light*, the CBS sudser dropped its *The* in 1975. TV's longest-running serial is now pushing seventy years old! Although it was drowning in Daytime Emmy accolades in 2006, the once glorious *GL* is nevertheless struggling in the Nielsen ratings, and suffering from budget cutbacks as a result. But there's still plenty to love about the continuing saga of the super-rich Spauldings, the nouveau riche Lewises, the middle-class Bauers, and the spunky Coopers.

SIGNATURE SUPERCOUPLE: Jonathan Randall and Tammy Winslow (Tom Pelphrey, Stephanie Gatschet). Their mothers are half-sisters, which makes them first cousins. Or is it half-cousins? Anyway, they're definitely kissin' cousins. Some call them icky, others call Jonathan and Tammy's forbidden love too hot to be stopped.

TOWN SAINT: Nurse Lillian Raines (Tina Sloan). Yes, she committed adultery with Dr. Ed Bauer (Peter Simon) but Lil felt *really* guilty about it afterward.

TOWN SLUT: Reva Shayne Lewis. Since the '80s, Kim Zimmer has played the self-proclaimed "Slut of Springfield" with an inimitable bluster, charm, and sass. Reva's soulmate is the Oklahoma-born oilman Joshua Lewis (Robert Newman), but that didn't stop her from marrying Josh's alcoholic brother Billy (Jordan Clarke), and their father H.B. (the late Larry Gates).

TOWN STUD: Joshua Lewis. Reva's classy, handsome, true blue "Bud" just gets better with age.

TOWN PSYCHO: Dinah Marler. As played by Gina Tognoni, she's a hot-tempered, homicidal hussy with a wry sense of humor and touching vulnerability. This Dinah-mite character is the No. 1 reason to watch GL these days.

One Life to Live

DEBUT: July 15, 1968, on ABC

SETTING: Llanview, Pennsylvania

HERE'S THE SITCH: Created by Agnes Nixon—two years before she gave us *All My Children*—this dark drama focuses on the multiethnic web of family and friends of long-suffering heiress Victoria "Viki" Lord (Erika Slezak). Among the most fascinating ones to watch are her half- brother Todd Manning (Trevor St. John), a semi-reformed rapist, who simultaneously wages love and war with semi-reformed bitch, Blair Cramer (Kassie DePaiva); Viki's daughter, Jessica (Bree Williamson), who has inherited her mother's multiple-personality issues; and Viki's archrival, Dorian Lord (Robin Strasser). "I love *One Life to Live* because when you find yourself in Llanview, there's no confusion that you're in some other town at some other time," Strasser says. "Our show doesn't look like anybody else's shows. We're not as easily confused as some other show are with each other." Too right, Robin!

SIGNATURE SUPERCOUPLE: Viki Lord and Clint Buchanan (Jerry Ver Dorn). Sure, they're divorced, but a romantic reunion is inevitable. Unless Dorian wins Clint for herself!

TOWN SAINT: Evangeline "Vangie" Williamson (Renée Elise Goldsberry). This beautiful, heroic African-American attorney is a survivor who never quits fighting for our rights. Even when a crazed serial killer kidnaps her, dresses her up in a cheerleader outfit, and sets her on fire. Or when she's blinded by a tornado. Or when . . .

TOWN SLUT: Renee Divine Buchanan (Patricia Elliott). Sure, she's the respectable proprietress of Llanview's posh Palace Hotel now. But fans haven't forgotten that Renee met her billionaire cowboy husband, Asa Buchanan (Phil Carey), back when she was the presiding madam of a brothel in Nevada!

TOWN STUD: Seriously, who can choose just one? Though Latin lover Antonio Vega (Kamar de los Reyes) is really sporting some impressive abs lately.

TOWN PSYCHO: Though she's generally regarded as the town saint, Viki Lord has many sinful demons inside her. Since the '60s, she has struggled with DID (dissociative identity disorder) as a result of the traumatizing sexual abuse she suffered at the hands of her evil father, the late newspaper baron Victor Lord. The most famous of Viki's six alternate personalities is Niki Smith, the lowbrow, selfish, slutty antithesis of everything good and decent that Viki stands for. Brava Niki!

Passions

DEBUT: July 5, 1999, on NBC

SETTING: Harmony, New England

HERE'S THE SITCH: Created by James E. Reilly, the youngest of today's daytime soaps tells stories of desperate, obsessive love in the coastal New England town of Harmony. Reilly is best known for the camp humor and supernatural storytelling he used to boost *Days of our Lives*'s ratings in the '90s. (He's the auteur responsible for the aforementioned live burial and demonic possession tales.) Tabitha Lenox, the resident 300-year-old witch played by Juliet Mills, watches over Harmony's heartaches with sinister delight: Theresa Lopez-Fitzgerald Crane (Lindsay Korman Hartley) wants Ethan Winthrop (Eric Martsolf), Luis Lopez-Fitzgerald (Galen Gering) wants Sheridan Crane (McKenzie Westmore), Ivy Winthrop (Kim Johnston Ulrich) wants Sam Bennett (James Hyde), and nobody can be happy. Not even poor Whitney Russell (Brooke Kerr), who became a novitiate nun after having an incest baby with her supposed half-brother, Chad Harris (Charles Divins).

SIGNATURE SUPERCOUPLE: Theresa Lopez-Fitzgerald Crane and Ethan Winthrop

TOWN SAINT: Sheridan Crane. Rather like Viki on *One Life to Live*, Sheridan is a saintly heiress who's tormented by her twisted, powerful daddy, Alistair Crane (John Reilly). Early in the series, Sheridan was said to have been friends with the late Princess Diana, a fellow "candle in the wind."

TOWN SLUT: Rebecca Hotchkiss Crane. As played by redheaded rascal Andrea Evans—who gained '80s fame as *One Life to Live*'s Tina Lord—Rebecca is the hilarious harlot of Harmony's high society who uses her curvaceous body to get whatever she wants.

TOWN STUD: Luis Lopez-Fitzgerald. With his muscular frame, gorgeous head of black hair, and those thick, long eyelashes, Galen Gering has been stirring viewers' *Passions* since day one.

TOWN PSYCHO: Norma Bates (Marianne Muellerleile). This burly, ax-wielding mental case in denim overalls is *Passions*'s female answer to Norman Bates, the titular murderer played by Anthony Perkins in Alfred Hitchcock's 1960 classic *Psycho*. Of course, Norma is far more butch than Norman ever was. Although Norma's sexual orientation has never been officially established, she strongly suggests a bull dyke. Her penchant for singing "I've Written a Letter to Daddy"—in full Bette-Davis-as-Baby-Jane drag—is also highly questionable. Norma's recent visit to a lesbian bar suggests she might *finally* be cracking open her closet door. Hey, maybe some day she'll find a Goth chick that's turned on by that crusty old human skull she carries around!

The Young and the Restless

DEBUT: March 26, 1973, on CBS
SETTING: Genoa City, Wisconsin
HERE'S THE SITCH: Created by Lee Phillip and William

J. Bell, *Y&R* has been the No. 1–rated daytime soap on the air for a long time. Clever writing, fabulously upscale production values and a superb cast keep us glued to the continuing stories of the Abbott, Newman, Chancellor, and Winters families. Although the real Genoa City, Wisconsin is a small town with a population of less than 3,000, *Y&R*'s version is a mid-size city with a burgeoning cosmetics industry! The show liberally mixes romantic intrigues with corporate in-fighting. A typical episode features someone jockeying for the CEO position at Newman Enterprises, while someone else sees a doctor to determine her baby's paternity.

SIGNATURE SUPERCOUPLE: Nikki and Victor Newman (Melody Thomas Scott, Eric Braeden)

TOWN SAINT: Cassie Newman (Camryn Grimes). Ever since the beloved teenager died too young in a car accident, Genoa City's sinful adults invoke Cassie's memory whenever they need strength to set aside their petty squabbles.

TOWN SLUT: Phyllis Summers Abbott (Michelle Stafford). Like most soap redheads, she's got a fiery personality—and an eye for other women's husbands. Her raunchy affair with rich boy Nicholas Newman (Joshua Morrow) is the hottest scandal in *Y&R*'s recent history.

TOWN STUD: That title is shared by Bradley Carlton (Don Diamont), Nicholas Newman, Paul Williams (Doug Davidson), and Neil Winters (Kristoff St. John). Read more about them in the Top 10 Soap Hunks chapter.

GONE BUT NOT FORGOTTEN

THE CANCELLATION of a soap opera is like a death in the family to many suds fans. Thanks to daily reruns on SOAPnet, these three axed daytime dramas are still around to comfort loyal fans and even earn a few new ones.

ANOTHER WORLD: Cancelled in 1999 after thirty-five years on NBC, this serial followed the lives, loves, and outrageously big hairdos of Bay City. Read more about *AW*'s memorable characters in the Top 10 Soap Divas chapter.

RYAN'S HOPE: Created by acclaimed soap scribes Claire Labine and Paul Mayer, *RH* spun its domestic drama around a lower-middle-class Irish-American family in New York City. Watch a few classic episodes and you'll understand why soap purists fervently wish Ms. Labine would please come out of retirement.

PORT CHARLES: This half-hour *General Hospital* spin-off was never very successful, but it got quite interesting when it switched to a Spanish telenovela format and began copying supernatural themes from shows like *Passions, Dark Shadows,* and *Buffy the Vampire Slayer*. Plus, it featured *Baywatch* babe and *Dancing with the Stars* champ, Kelly Monaco, playing twins!

Soap Towns Quiz

#2

QUIZ

1. Which soap-opera town was flooded during an infamous "Shock Wave" story line?

   a. *Harmony, New England*
   b. *Genoa City, Wisconsin*
   c. *Pine Valley, Pennsylvania*
   d. *Sunset Beach, California*

2. Which soap featured an underground city called Eterna?

   a. One Life to Live
   b. Passions
   c. Strange Paradise
   d. Dark Shadows

Soap Towns Quiz

3. Which defunct soap was set in Crowder, Virginia?

    a. The Egg and I
    b. Full Circle
    c. Bright Promise
    d. Search for Tomorrow

4. Where did the characters on ABC's *Loving* reside?

    a. *New York City*
    b. *Santa Barbara, California*
    c. *Corinth*
    d. *Fernwood, Ohio*

5. Which early soap centered around astronauts and their wives in Cape Canaveral, Florida?

    a. *Morning Star*
    b. *Emerald Point, N.A.S.*
    c. *The Brighter Day*
    d. *The Clear Horizon*

TOWN PSYCHO: Sheila Carter (Kimberlin Brown). All this psychotic former nurse wants is love and acceptance, but she doesn't quite realize that poisoning, baby switching, and paternity-test tampering are not the best ways to endear oneself to others. Sheila's terror sprees on *Y&R* and its sister soap *B&B* are the stuff of soap legend.

ALISON SWEENEY PLAYS SALEM'S SCHEMING SAMI BRADY ON NBC'S *DAYS OF OUR LIVES*. (COURTESY OF NBC UNIVERSAL)

CHAPTER THREE

Why Daytime Is Gaytime

QUOTE

"I'm not letting you watch that show anymore!"

AS YOU read in Soap History 101, soap operas were essentially created to feed the romantic fantasies of heterosexual housewives and sell them household goods during the commercials. So how did so many gay folks become soap-opera addicts?

We all remember how we got sucked into the suds. For me, it was a sudden *Dynasty* obsession at age eleven. This little gay boy wanted to be Alexis Morell Carrington Colby Dexter Rowan when I grew up. That Joan Collins had such a diva-licious English accent, when she scolded Joseph the snotty majordomo, calling him an "impotent voyeur." The beautiful bitch also had so many glamorous clothes and sexy boyfriends and husbands. I was her slave. Then came that harrowing cliffhanger episode where my Alexis lost control of her car and drove off a bridge.

I shrieked at the sight of this all too mortal goddess plunging into her watery grave. My mother—who was in the kitchen chatting on the telephone—came rushing into the living room to see what was the matter. She found me there on my knees in front of the TV, shaking and sobbing.

"Alexis is dead!" I cried.

"I'm not letting you watch that show anymore!"

Mommy's threat was an idle one, for the poor lady knew I would go all Alexis on her if she ever came between me and my *Dynasty* Wednesday nights on ABC.

With my appetite for drama whetted, I started tuning into soaps, instead of cartoons, when I came home from school in the afternoons. Instead of just on Wednesdays, the sudsy fun happened five days a week, fifty-two weeks a year. In daytime, I found there was no season-ending cliffhanger that left you in suspense all summer long, and there was no beginning, middle, or end. Because the stories were continuous, they went on forever and ever, for all the *Days of our Lives*. There was always fantasy, there was always romance, there was always lots of money, and no one ever died. Well, some did, but most of the dead just came back from the grave in a few years, either as themselves or a long-lost look-alike played by the same actor.

For children of divorced couples, like me, the family aspect of soaps was just as appealing as the romance, if not more so. My home and school lives were both rather tumultuous. As a bookish gay boy who didn't happen to enjoy playing sports or chasing girls, I didn't fit in. So I found shelter by escaping into a fantasy world where misfits are celebrated. Core families like *Days*'s Bradys and Hortons, *Guiding Light*'s Bauers, Lewises, and Spauldings, and *One Life to Live*'s Buchanans and Cramers, were always there, forgiving and loving all the black sheep of their families, no matter how different or outrageous they were. How comforting, right?

It's also fun to watch fellow underdogs go through life's struggles and triumph (at least some of the time) through spunk, creativity, and resourcefulness (particularly if the underdog we're watching is one of our favorite soap divas). "Every gay man has his female companion, also known as a fag hag, and soaps are often an extension of that," chuckles Dustin Cushman, founder of SoapFan.com. "There is often one female on the show we pick as our favorite to latch on to, someone we'd want to be friends with in real life."

For many *Days of our Lives* fans, that best gal pal is Samantha "Sami" Brady, who is superbly played by Alison Sweeney. The lonely, wisecracking Sami constantly schemes to attain the loving relationship, the happy family, and the sense of belonging she so desperately craves. Naturally, since it's a soap, she usually takes her efforts way too far and anyone in Sami's way gets hurt.

"Gay guys really like villainesses," Sweeney enthuses. "They definitely see Sami's side more than her perfect older sister, Carrie's. I think gay people relate to Sami because it's so hard for them to deal with society. You're always being stereotyped and you're always having to justify your lifestyle to people. I feel like, in some ways, Sami has that in common! She's like, 'Look, I just want

Soap Families

1. Which *Guiding Light* family is famous for the melodramatic fireworks at their annual Fourth of July barbecue?

   a. The Spauldings
   b. The Lewises
   c. The Coopers
   d. The Bauers

2. What is Grandma Alice Horton's specialty dish on *Days of our Lives*?

   a. Lemon meringue pie
   b. Powdered doughnuts
   c. Jamaican jerk chicken
   d. Salem Surprise

3. Which *General Hospital* clan owned the Triple L Diner?

   a. The Quartermaines
   b. The Cassadines
   c. The Spencers
   d. The Scorpios

Soap Families

4. Which Hollywood star never played a Ryan family member on *Ryan's Hope*?

    a. *Marg Helgenberger*
    b, *Yasmine Bleeth*
    c. *Kate Mulgrew*
    d. *Christian Slater*
    e. *Richard Backus*

5. Which hunky father has the most living, biological children on *The Young and the Restless*?

    a. *Victor Newman*
    b. *Jack Abbott*
    c. *John Abbott*
    d. *Neil Winters*

to live my life and be happy. Can you butt out already?'

"The other great reason why people relate to Sami is that her life blows up in her face, and she literally gets humiliated in front of the entire town all the time," Sweeney says with a laugh. "She gets embarrassed and humiliated and she actually picks herself up, dusts herself off, and tries again. You have to have admiration for someone who can stay living in that town of Salem for thirteen years after being continuously humiliated!"

"Yeah, *Days* definitely plays to the drama and we always try to do great wardrobe, hairstyles, stunts, and stories," she says. "But for all of its crazy shenanigans and whatnot, the roots are in reality. That's what I love about this genre."

I couldn't have said it more eloquently. Basically, our soaps are a sumptuous multi-course meal of emotional comfort food. We laugh, we cry, we relate and we feast on the tasty eye candy for dessert. Whether you're gay, straight, or somewhere in between, the daytime soaps have something special to serve up, and everyone at the table is an honored guest.

DOES IT GET ANY BETTER THAN A SHIRTLESS STUD
WITH THE PECS TO PROVE IT? AUSTIN PECK PLAYS
"AUSTIN REED" ON *DAYS OF OUR LIVES*. (COURTESY
OF NBC UNIVERSAL)

CHAPTER FOUR

Top 10 Soap Hunks

QUOTE

"I was wearing nothing but vines over my crotch in every scene!"

WARNING: The author strongly recommends enjoying this chapter alone, with a cold beverage in hand. You may require something to cool yourself down while perusing this hot countdown of the ten sexiest hunks in daytime TV history. The "alone" part is just in case that frosty drink isn't enough to keep overheated readers from feeling compelled to take something else in hand. If it happens, honey, don't be ashamed. You would hardly be the first soap fan to appreciate the ab-liciousness of these afternoon delights with the curtains drawn.

#10: Gordon Thomson

WHY HE'S HOT: Gordon Thomson's signature soap role was Adam Carrington, the long lost son of

Alexis and Blake Carrington (Joan Collins, John Forsythe) on *Dynasty*. Dark-haired, debonair, and deliciously diabolical, Adam ironically held more appeal for homo fans than his gay brother, Steven (who was played first by Al Corley, then Jack Coleman). Perhaps it was because Steven was a passive, people-pleasing goody two shoes, while Adam looked and behaved just like a male version of his fabulously feisty mother, Alexis. Bitchy barbs, scandalous schemes, and '80s greed were the ambitious Adam's best qualities. Because he wasn't raised as a Carrington, Adam felt like an outsider and had to work for his parents' love and approval just as much as his gay bro.

Gordon's Greatest Daytime Deeds

Before and after *Dynasty*, Thomson spent many years in the daytime suds. Here's a rundown of his favorite roles.

RYAN'S HOPE: "I did *Ryan's Hope* for thirteen weeks in 1981-82. I played that well-known Egyptologist, Aristotle Benedict White. What happened was that [*RH* writer] Claire Labine had been to Egypt on a summer holiday, fell in love with the place and the extraordinary history of the Pharaohs, and she wanted to get that on her show in New York. Faith (Karen Morris Gowdy) was the image of an old Egyptian princess and Aristotle fell in love with her. Eventually, he was murdered. It was not a very good story. The set decorator, Sy Tomashoff, did a really brilliant job of recreating a tomb and a sarcophagus. But the heart of the show was the Ryan family and you cannot bring in such a piece of exotica. It was like when we had the aliens abduct Fallon (Emma Samms) on *Dynasty*! What an asinine idea! I worked with a couple of really good actors who thought the whole thing was so silly; they couldn't keep a straight face. That made life rather difficult."

SANTA BARBARA: "I was the third actor to play Mason Capwell. Lane Davies created the part. It made him a star, but he didn't like doing it, although they were very generous about giving him tons of time off to do Shakespeare. Then Terry Lester took over for one year and he hated it, too. Then [veteran soap producer] John Conboy was looking around for somebody who was dark who could play Mason and lit on my name. It was practically the best part I've ever had! Mason was a judge who had a great, sardonic sense of humor. He's capable of great sarcasm and had a great vocabulary. He was smart, funny, and passionate. I used to get mail from lawyers who loved the show. I think Mason and Julia (Nancy Lee Grahn) made up one of the more interesting couples in daytime history. They were so smart! "

SUNSET BEACH: "I played AJ Deschanel. I loved the name. He was mad about Olivia, who was played by [British actress] Lesley Anne Down."

#9: Michael Corbett

WHY HE'S HOT: In the '80s, Michael Corbett stood among daytime's best hunks you loved to hate. "I was on daytime for twenty years and I was always sleeping with two relatives at the same time," says the onetime *Playgirl Presents Soap Hunks* cover boy. "On *Ryan's Hope*, I was with a mother and her daughter. On *Search for Tomorrow*, it was two sisters. On *The Young and the Restless*, I married a rich woman, then I married her mother, and I had a girlfriend on the side!"

HIS SOAPY CAREER: Michael Pavel, *Ryan's Hope*, 1979-81; Warren Carter, *Search for Tomorrow*, 1982-85; David Kimball, *The Young and the Restless*, 1986-2000

Hot Stuff!

"Soap-opera hairdos were very big and feathery in the '80s, even for guys," Corbett recalls with mock horror. "I had fluffy wings in my hair, like John Travolta or Farrah Fawcett. But my story lines were really good! Granted, I had to play a lot of them in a bathing suit or in bed, but I always had great stuff to play as the manipulative cad."

LIFE AFTER DAYTIME: Since his soap days, Corbett has gone into TV hosting. He's an entertainment correspondent on *Extra* and serves as host and producer of the syndicated TV series *Mansions &*

Millionaires. He also writes how-to books about real estate. As the former soap scumball jokes: "People are calling me the home wrecker turned home renovator."

#8: Tuc Watkins

WHY HE'S HOT: With his chiseled looks and killer comic timing, the lucky Tuc Watkins gets to be a brilliant character actor who looks like a hunky leading man. He's best known to soap fans as *One Life to Live*'s grifter with a heart of gold, David Vickers. Unlike a lot of macho soap studs that prefer to look "cool" and be the alpha dog in their scenes, Watkins isn't afraid to take chances with the daffy David. "Take Cary Grant from his classic movies and combine him with Kevin Kline from *A Fish Called Wanda,* and you've got David Vickers," jokes the actor. "He's the debonair guy and he's the fool. When I started on *One Life to Live*, I was supposed to be this cool, mysterious character—I just wasn't very good at it. I realized one day when David fell down the stairs that *that's* what my character should be. I just try to look for 'Where is it funny?' I think it's what differentiates David from other soap characters. That's not what you usually see in our medium. The response I've gotten from men, women, gays, straights—and even some Russians— has been really positive."

MY SECRET SHAME: Tuc Watkins sympathizes with his gay soap fans, since we have to come out twice—as gays and as soap fans! "Soap fans probably have a lot in common with gay people, because they constantly have to out themselves and say, 'Yes, I'm a fan of soap operas.' There are some common threads there. I think most people would be more comfortable saying 'I buy pornography' than saying 'I watch soap operas.' There's that much of a stigma about being a soap fan!"

Stuck on Tuc

TUC'S FULL NAME is Charles Curtis Watkins III. He hails from Kansas.

TUC'S FAVORITE SOAPY LOVE INTEREST was Robin Strasser, who plays *One Life to Live*'s devious diva, Dorian Lord. David Vickers is one of Dorian's many ex-husbands, but *One Life* fans think of D & D as a couple even when they're seeing other people. "Playing David without Dorian is like playing with matches without gasoline," Tuc quips. "It's fun, but it lacks showmanship."

TUC STARRED ON SHOWTIME'S SUDSY SATIRE *Beggars and Choosers*. "It was like the movie Network," he says. "I played Malcolm Laffley, a television casting executive [at fictional network LGT]. I wanted to play Malcolm because I thought he was a multifaceted character—he started out as a gay guy in the closet and then came out. He was also a fun character because he had a sense of humor."

TUC SPOOFED SUDSERS as Sterling Scott, a vain but good-natured soap-opera hunk in the 1997 gay indie comedy *I Think I Do*. Sterling is the boyfriend of Bob, as played by Alexis Arquette, who's rather cute out of drag!

IN BETWEEN STINTS on *One Life to Live*, Watkins played a drug-dealing doctor on *General Hospital*. "Pierce Dorman was a lot of fun," Tuc recalls, "because he was an extreme character. He was nothing but evil and that's fun to play just because you can go so over the top with it—kind of like Gary Oldman in every movie that he does." Among his sins was planting heroin in the chest cavity of a cadaver in the morgue!

#7: Kerr Smith

WHY HE'S HOT: In 1996, Kerr Smith made his acting debut on *As the World Turns* as rebellious teen Theodore "Ryder" Hughes. His character's childhood nickname was Teddy, but Ryder sounded more butch to the soap's writers. In his first scene, they had the leather-jacketed hottie mount a motorcycle and ride up poolside at the posh Oakdale Country Club. Scandalized socialites clutched their pearls! But with his pretty-boy looks, bedroom eyes, and sweet nature, Ryder was really more of a Teddy bear than a bad boy after all. During his year in Oakdale, Ryder romanced a cop's daughter, Nikki Munson, who was played by future movie starlet Jordana Brewster (*The Fast and the Furious*). When that fizzled out, Smith went on to sizzle in primetime TV and films.

GAY FOR PAY: Smith made homo history during his five years on the WB's *Dawson's Creek* as gay good guy Jack McPhee. Who could forget *Dawson's* touching third-season finale in 2000? Aptly entitled "True Love," this episode featured Jack passionately kissing his boyfriend, Ethan (Adam Kauffman). In so doing, they pulled off the biggest queer TV event since Ellen came out. Better yet, the *Creek* series finale in 2003 allowed viewers to glimpse the Capeside kids' lives five years in the future. The real shocker? Michelle Williams's Jen dies young and her infant daughter is adopted by her best friend Jack and his life partner—Pacey's policeman brother, Doug! Much to our delight, Pacey's long-held suspicions about his brother's sexual orientation were confirmed. A soapy side note: Doug was portrayed by Dylan Neal, who had previously starred on *The Bold and the Beautiful* as Dylan Shaw, a ripped dude who worked his way through college as a stripper. *Mmm* . . . as the song goes, I don't see nothin' wrong with a little bump and grind.

AFTER THE SOAPS: Smith spiced up the fantasy/horror genre with roles in *Final Destination, The Forsaken*, and the WB's witch-fest *Charmed*, where he played FBI agent Kyle Brody. Later, he played legal eagles on NBC's Pentagon drama Pentagon drama *E-Ring* and Fox's *Justice*.

#6: Joshua Morrow

WHY HE'S HOT: Joshua Morrow has spent twelve years playing rich boy Nicholas Newman on *The Young and the Restless*. His intense eyes, pouty lips, and frequent shirtless scenes have earned him major soap hunk status. "I'm not one of those guys who's like, 'Don't call me a hunk. Please take me seriously as an actor!'" Morrow says with a laugh. "It's part of the job to take my clothes off, so I'm not gonna dispute it if you want to call me that. It's better than making me your cover boy for a top 10 dorks list. Although I would be honored by that as well!"

HE'S GAY FRIENDLY: "One of my best friends in the world is gay and I love him more than anything," says Morrow, who appreciates *Y&R*'s queer fans. "The more people that appreciate what I do and, I guess, how I look, the better. It's always a compliment. As actors, we are always looking for some reinforcement and validation."

HIS GAYEST STORYLINE: Back in Nick's days at Genoa City High, he and his future wife, Sharon (Sharon Case), were crowned king and queen of the Big Kahuna Dance. "That was definitely the gayest scenario I've ever been in," Morrow chuckles. "Several guys had to wander around close to naked in floral loincloths. This would be an atmosphere that gay dudes might enjoy. I definitely thought that while it was happening!"

NOT VERY 'N SYNC: In the '90s, Morrow formed a short-lived boy band called 3Deep with Canadian musician CJ Huyer and dimpled TV heartthrob Eddie Cibrian, who played teen rapist Matt Clark on *Y&R*. "We did two albums, went on tour in a van and drank beer," he recalls. "For me, it was all about fun and seeing how it felt to be a pop star. It was just a big party for two years. I never considered myself a real musician. Hell no!"

#5: Cameron Mathison

WHY HE'S HOT: Canadian import Cameron Mathison joined *All My Children* in 1998 as hot-tempered hero Ryan Lavery. Perhaps the most ab-licious actor in daytime soaps today, he sports an eight-pack on par with any muscle mag model. The quintessential model-turned-actor, he brazenly mugs and poses for the camera, but tries to sound a bit humble about his hotness in press interviews. "I've had some weird, silly moments on *AMC*," he has said. "Ryan's been stuck in the elevator on his way to work and he undresses! I don't mind [going shirtless] as long as it makes sense." To Cam's flesh-hungry fans, there's really no time it *doesn't* make sense. Happily, the dude's famous for his crowd-pleasing habit of whipping off his shirt at public appearances. "We call this guy 'Assmuffins Mathison,'" jokes co-star Jeff Branson, who plays Ryan's brother, Jonathan. "Cam's got buns of steel and, seriously, he's built like a concrete wall. He's like a magnet for attention. But there's not a nicer dude on the planet and he's the first to laugh at himself about it. He gets the craziest fan mail with panties and naked pictures from girls *and* guys!"

SOWING THE SEEDS OF LOVE: Several of *AMC*'s breeder babes have gone to lots of trouble to get pregnant by Pine Valley's hottest specimen of manhood. Oh, and speaking of Ryan Lavery's male specimens . . . "In the beginning of my stint on the show," Mathison says, "Ryan made a donation to the sperm bank because he thought he was God's gift to women and all of them should have a shot at it. That was a fun story line to do."

I LOVE THE NIGHTLIFE: Mathison made his big-screen debut in *54* as—what else?—a bare-chested bartender at the infamous New York City club, Studio 54. Covered in body glitter, he served up cocktails alongside the film's star Ryan Phillippe, who once played gay teen Billy Douglas on *One Life to Live*.

I WANT MY REALITY TV: In addition to his work on *AMC*, soap fans know Mathison as the hunky host of SOAPnet's reality-TV casting call, *I Wanna Be a Soap Star*.

#4: Kristoff St. John

WHY HE'S HOT: Kristoff St. John is daytime's answer to Denzel Washington. This man is sex appeal, intelligence, and dignity all rolled into one irresistible package. In 1989, he started off in soaps as Adam Marshall, the resident heartthrob on NBC's short-lived drama, *Generations*. It was the first network sudser to feature a largely African-American cast. Shortly after that show's cancellation, St. John joined *The Young and the Restless* in 1991 as Neil Winters, a rising young business executive, and he's been there ever since. "I'm coming up on two decades in daytime television," he says with a smile. "I'm no flash in the pan! I feel privileged to be one of the mainstays on Y&R and on daytime. It's an honor I wear with a lot of pride."

BLACK IS BEAUTIFUL: St. John's TV wife is Victoria Rowell, the former *Diagnosis Murder* star who plays Drucilla Barber Winters on *Y&R*. Dru has grown up from a trash-talking, illiterate street punk to a ballerina, supermodel, and business executive in her own right. "She has sex appeal and sass appeal," Kristoff points out with a laugh. Together St. John and Rowell have become celebrated black icons, partly because their daily work counteracts negative images of African-Americans in pop culture. Rowell has won ten Image Awards for outstanding actress in a daytime drama from the NAACP (National Association for the Advancement of Colored People) and St. John has won six for outstanding actor. "Neil and Dru are a respectful and refined couple," St. John says. "That Image Award doesn't lose its luster. Every time I receive it, I still get the chicken skin, the goose bumps, and the lump in the throat. I realize I've done something right for another year on my favorite job. The Image Award is just what the name says. It's not just your character's image, but also your professional image as an artist, and I dig that. Those awards have a welcome place in my family's house."

MY BROTHER'S KEEPER: The sexy Shemar Moore played Neil's bad-boy brother, Malcolm Winters, from 1994-2002 and then again from 2004-05. He's since found primetime success on CBS's *Criminal Minds*. "Honestly, if you want to know the number one statement that I've heard from fans, it's 'Where's your brother? We love you Neil, but where's Malcolm?' That doesn't surprise me and doesn't offend me at all because Shemar's a beautiful man. He gives great face. It was nice to share the *Y&R* stage with him for as long as I did. I love my boy. He's really like my little brother. It's nice to watch him leave the nest and do something with his career. That makes me so proud. I've heard from both straight and gay fans that the Neil character is the marrying kind, and Malcolm is more the one-night stand kind. So they want to sleep with Shemar Moore and have me as their life partner!"

GAY FOR PAY: St. John played a gay character in 2005's straight-to-DVD comedy, *Carpool Guy*, which featured a cast of popular daytime soap actors. The director was *L.A. Law* star Corbin Bernsen, who is the son of *Y&R*'s Jeanne Cooper. "When Corbin told me he had a part for me in his new movie, I said yes," St. John recalls. "He said, 'Wait, don't you want to see a script?' I said, 'I respect you and I want to be part of your directorial debut. I accept the challenge.' He said, 'OK, so you're gonna be playing a gay man.' I said, 'Fine, is that all?'" In the film, St. John's character, Steven, is the gay best friend of Hope (*Y&R*'s Lauralee Bell). The running joke is that Hope's husband, Joel (*General Hospital*'s Rick Hearst), suspects Steven of faking his homosexuality just to cozy up to Hope and seduce her. "I didn't do a method acting thing where I hung out with gay guys in West Hollywood or anything, but I wanted to be as natural and believable as possible, not too over the top," he explains. "We did do a silly scene where I come out of the bathroom in Joel's bathrobe, his slippers, and a towel [rolled up like a turban] on my head! My line was, 'I'm gay. I'm not after your wife.' Then in the end, we decipher that my character is possibly straight or bisexual and maybe he was after Joel's wife. We don't know for sure. It was a challenging part because I hadn't yet played a gay man. I just wanted to be believable and not offend anyone, so I hope that I accomplished that goal." No worries, Kristoff. Your scene stealing antics brought us big laughs.

#3: Jesse Metcalfe

WHY HE'S HOT: California-grown stud puppy Jesse Metcalfe has a pretty boy's face and a pumped, muscular body that's *all man*. It's rather apropos that his middle name is Eden, since he's just as tempting as the forbidden fruit in the biblical garden his parents named him after! (Hey, gushing praise is OK if it's totally true.) Metcalfe aroused our nation's adoration as John, the teenage gardener who was famously seduced by married temptress Gabrielle Solis (Eva Longoria) on ABC's hit nighttime sudser *Desperate Housewives*. "That's because he has his shirt off every episode," Longoria has said. "The day Jesse walked in, everybody's mouth dropped. He has sexual energy oozing out of his pores." Recently, Metcalfe made his sizzling big screen debut as the titular horndog in *John Tucker Must Die*.

THE DESPERATE GARDENER'S DAYTIME ROOTS: Whenever friends drool over Metcalfe, we daytimers can't help but feel he's *our* sudsy stud. It's only fair since we saw him first! Before he gained fame on

Wisteria Lane, Metcalfe quit New York University's Tisch School of the Arts to take advantage of his big break—a contract role on NBC's supernatural soap, *Passions*. He spent five years in the uber-kooky town of Harmony as the heroic Miguel Lopez-Fitzgerald. Miguel was hopelessly in love with Charity Standish (Molly Stanton), a syrupy-sweet blonde, who didn't realize that she had mysterious powers that threatened Evil's very existence. Sinister sorceress Tabitha (Juliet Mills) was always trying to kill the young couple, since the chaste Charity would come into her full powers if she ever lost her virginity to her true love. Yes, *really*. So rather than run for his life like any real dude would, Miguel was steadfastly loyal to Charity, despite the lack of sex and the serious perils involved in dating her. Like Zombie Charity, the look-alike who schemed to seduce him into eternal damnation. And the witch who rigged the town's Christmas tree to electrocute him. Or the giant satanic serpent that carried him off into the flames of Hell in its bloodthirsty jaws. Naturally, Miguel visited the damned denizens of Hades with a bare torso, as usual! "We basically had to laugh while we were doing those scenes because it was so ridiculous at times," Metcalfe said in 2001. "I've had no shirt on for three weeks. The fact that Miguel is running through Hell, half dressed, looking for his girlfriend was pretty comedic." Yeah, but it was hellaciously hot, too.

#2 Christopher Reeve

WHY HE'S HOT: The late Christopher Reeve's many fans would agree it's not too effusive to call him a model of male perfection. Standing at 6' 4" and sporting jet-black hair and cerulean blue eyes, he was not only S.M.T.—"*So* my type!"—he was the heartthrob of girls and gays everywhere in the 1970s and '80s. Later in his life, the pop culture icon was unfortunately rendered quadriplegic in a horseback-riding accident and became a real-life superhero as a spokesperson for the disabled, and an activist on behalf of stem-cell research.

HE STARTED ON SOAPS: Before Reeve donned Kal-El's cape and leotard for 1978's *Superman*, he played bigamist Ben Harper on CBS's long-running serial *Love of Life*. Ben was a sexy ski bum who turned into a greedy gigolo after his rich bitch mama cut him off financially. "The guy had lots of money and no moral scruples whatsoever," Reeve recalled in a 1981 interview. "He was married to two women at the same time, one of whom was pregnant, and the Mafia had a contract out on him because of some blackmail extortion scheme." Reeve exited the soap when Ben found his conscience at last, confessed to his crimes, and went to prison.

CHRIS'S CAREER CLONE: Just like Christopher Reeve, *Superman Returns* hunk Brandon Routh did a brief stint on daytime TV, then went on to become an overnight sensation by playing Supes on the big screen. Routh and Reeve even played very similar soap characters. On *One Life to Live*, Routh was Seth Anderson, a gold digger with boyish, all American good looks, who two-timed heiress Jessica Buchanan with her scheming slut of a sister, Natalie. A guilty Seth later renounced his wicked ways and left Llanview. Sounds just like Ben Harper's sordid story on *Love of Life*! Oh, and notice how Routh and Reeve both starred on soap operas with the word *Life* in their titles. Spooky, huh?

#1: Austin Peck

WHY HE'S HOT: Since his 1995 daytime debut, the perpetually shirtless Austin Peck—also known as "Austin Pecs"—has dazzled *Days of our Lives* fans. Gals and gays alike tune in to the NBC soap for a daily eyeful of his masculine charms. *Mmm* . . . who wouldn't drool at the sight of that terrific torso, adorned with abs of steel, powerful pectorals and perky, medallion-sized nipples?

WHY HE'S COOL: Peck could easily coast by on his looks. Instead, he brings a refreshing sense of humor to his portrayal of *Days* good guy Austin Reed. He often delivers lines in an ironic way that lets the audience know he knows his story lines are silly and the dialogue daft, but we should just go along for the fun of it. In photo shoots, the 34-year-old ex-model's big brown eyes dance with the potential of maximum mischief. And yeah, Peck knows he's hot, but he's well past having a big ego about it. "I stay in shape because I have a job on a soap opera, and I like to do it for my own health," he says. "The most irritating thing is when people assume that

I think I'm 'all that,' so they try to treat me as if I'm *not* all that, like they're going to be the ones to humble me." Laughing, he adds: "I'm married and have two kids! I get in fights with my wife, and I clean up [my kids'] poop and pee. I don't need any more humbling!"

AUSTIN ON HIS GAY FANS: "If gay men like me, then I know I'm doing something right!" Peck grins. "Having a modeling background, I love gay people. I've been around them since I can remember. I love their openness, their sensitivity, and their sense of style."

FUN FACTS: AUSTIN VS AUSTIN

AUSTIN BARES (ALMOST) ALL: Peck and *Days* costar Julianne Morris, who played Greta, were reimagined as Adam and Eve in a virtual reality version of the biblical Garden of Eden. "I was wearing nothing but vines over my crotch in every scene!" he recalls. "It was the most improbable, ridiculous story they have ever done. In my opinion, it was beyond even Marlena's devil possession. I decided if I could get through that, I could do anything." Peck's fans agreed. We simply enjoyed those scantily clad scenes with the sound off!

FUN FACTS

HAIRY VS. SMOOTH: While Peck's pecs are smooth, the hairy-chested Patrick Muldoon originally played Austin Reed, from 1992–95. "I don't have that much hair on my chest. I've got hair on my forearms and hairy ape legs, but not much on my chest, so I just shave off what I have," he confides. "I've got to take my hat off to Patrick Muldoon, though. It's been over ten years since he played Austin, and people are *still* comparing us. If people remember Patrick's body hair, that's kudos for him! As soon as the Lord grows more hair on my body, I'll let it show."

ALL ABOUT AUSTIN: Although Austin Reed's parents—the pervy Curtis Reed and ex-hooker Kate Roberts—were poor role models, this dude's as good as gold. He stuck by true love Carrie Brady when acid burns ruined her modeling career and left her feeling un-pretty. He sweetly puts up with Carrie's bitchy baby sister, Sami, who has spent *years* obsessively chasing him. (Who can blame her?) Oh, and Austin's also a multitasker. Before turning cosmetics tycoon, he worked as a boxer and a piano player!

BOYS ON THE SIDE

These heavenly hunks also deserve honorable mentions for brightening up our days.

BRYAN DATTILO, *DAYS OF OUR LIVES*: He started out in Salem as Lucas Roberts, a geeky loser in love who spent years coming in second to his hotter big brother, Austin (Austin Peck). But Dattilo got more handsome with age—and hit the gym big time!—so Lucas is finally giving Austin some serious competition. Says his co-star Alison Sweeney (Sami): "Nothing's funnier than the fact that Lucas was in a coma for three years and woke up totally ripped and muscular! He had a *major* turnaround. I guess they must've fed him steroids while he was in that coma."

STEVE BURTON, *GENERAL HOSPITAL*: He rode a wave into our hearts as an alien teen's sexy surfer boyfriend on the sitcom *Out of This World*. Now, Burton breaks hearts (and bones) as Jason Morgan, the *GH* hit man who wears a too-tight T-shirt for all occasions. The popular blond stud's blue eyes stare out at us from the covers of soap mags on a weekly basis, and all we can do is *swoon*.

TYLER CHRISTOPHER, *GENERAL HOSPITAL*: As Greek prince Nikolas Cassadine, he's all proper manners in polite company but a burly beast in the bedroom. Tyler's swarthy charm clearly captivates his female co-stars off screen, too. He wed Eva Longoria (she had a bit part on *GH* before *Desperate Housewives*), got engaged to Vanessa Marcil (ex-Brenda), and has dated Natalia Livingston (Emily).

MICHAEL EASTON, *ONE LIFE TO LIVE*: This long-haired loverboy was a '90s teen dream as *Days of our Lives*'s Tanner Scofield. Later, Easton sunk his teeth into his signature soap role as *Port Charles*'s Caleb, the most seductive vampire ever to haunt the daytime. (Sorry, Barnabas!) Most recently, he's been criminally hot as broody police detective John McBain on *One Live to Live*.

MARK COLLIER, *AS THE WORLD TURNS*: As Oakdale's resident contractor Mike Kasnoff, he fulfills fans' buff construction worker fantasies every day. Collier's aficionados are still e-mailing each other screen grabs from the episode where he flashed his bodacious backside during a steamy shower scene.

Q QUIZ

Soap Hunks

1. Which soap hunk won the contract role of *All My Children*'s Del Hunkle on a reality show in 2005?

    a. *Winsor Harmon*
    b. *Justin Bruening*
    c. *Alec Musser*
    d. *Jacob Young*

2. Which hairy-chested Capitol star spent the entire summer of 1982 shirtless on-screen?

    a. *Nicholas Walker (Sam "Trey" Clegg III)*
    b. *Christopher Durham (Matt McCandless)*
    c. *Mitch Brown (Dylan Ross)*
    d. *Grant Aleksander (D. J. Phillips)*

3. Who was the first hottie to show off his bare butt on a daytime soap?

    a. *Doug Davidson (Paul Williams,* The Young and the Restless*)*
    b. *Don Diamont (Bradley Carlton,* The Young and the Restless*)*
    c. *Fabio (Himself,* The Bold and the Beautiful*)*

    d. *Jameson Parker (Brad Vernon,* One Life to Live*)*

    e. *Mark Collier (Mike Kasnoff,* As the World Turns*)*

4. Which *muy caliente* Latino hunk has starred on his soap the longest?

    a. *Galen Gering (Luis Lopez-Fitzgerald,* Passions*)*

    b. *Kamar de los Reyes (Antonio Vega,* One Life to Live*)*

    c. *Mario Lopez (Dr. Christian Ramirez,* The Bold and the Beautiful*)*

    d. *Maurice Benard (Sonny Corinthos,* General Hospital

5. Who has never struck a pose (either nude or semi-nude) for *Playgirl* magazine?

    a. *Austin Peck (Austin Reed,* Days of our Lives*)*

    b. *Steve Bond (Jimmy Lee Holt,* General Hospital*)*

    c. *Shemar Moore (Malcolm Winters,* The Young and the Restless*)*

    d. *Josh Duhamel (Leo DuPres,* All My Children*)*

    e. *Jean Le Clerc (Jeremy Hunter,* All My Children*)*

NO OTHER DIVA DOES IT QUITE LIKE "ERICA KANE," AS PLAYED BY THE EMMY AWARD-WINNING SUSAN LUCCI, ON ABC'S *ALL MY CHILDREN*. (© YOLANDA PEREZ/ AMERICAN BROADCASTING COMPANIES, INC.)

CHAPTER FIVE

Top 10 Soap Divas

QUOTE

> "I put my hand on her shoulder and she put her hand over mine. I'll tell you, for people whose minds are pure, the Bible Belt really picked up on that fast!"

THE DIVAS of daytime are not ordinary, coffee-cup characters. That is to say, they are not content to passively sit around the kitchen table, sipping Sanka and gossiping about their families and friends. They are too busy living their own lives out loud! They are never seen cooking, cleaning, or raising children. They have staff to do that sort of thing, darling. Our divas are wild women on the go: They're kissing and making love to model-gorgeous men, trading sassy one-liners with their rivals, dressing like red-carpet fashionistas every day and excelling in glamorous careers (even though they seldom go to the office). They're powerful, independent rule breakers who refuse to conform to rigid societal expectations—and they survive and prosper at it. No wonder they've always been worshipped by the often bored, and isolated gay kids who grow up watching them at home. Our soap ladies seem to be telling us: "Someday, you too can be proud, free, and fabulous! Set your aims high, and let nothing stand between you and what you want." Um, at least that's the message *this* soap-diva-in-the-making heard. Here's a countdown of the top ten femme fatales who have schemed and dreamed their way into our hearts.

#10: Darlene Conley

WHY WE LOVE HER: Though she's mighty proud to be an Irish girl from Chicago's South Side, Darlene Conley says she just had to "escape from behind the iron lace curtains" to become an actress in Hollywood. While the redhead appeared in Alfred Hitchcock's classic thriller *The Birds* and guest-starred on TV series like *Gunsmoke* and *The Mary Tyler Moore Show*, Conley really found her niche on the CBS soaps. In the '80s, she created two of daytime's most memorable ballsy broads. The first was Rose DeVille, an unscrupulous black-market baby broker on *The Young and the Restless*. Later, she joined *Y&R*'s sister show, *The Bold and the Beautiful*, as feisty fashion mogul Sally Spectra. "Sally Spectra is one of the most fascinating characters in daytime or nighttime or any other time!" Conley enthuses. "Gay fans love Sally primarily for her theatricality. I have always loved being around gay men and talking to them because they admire Sally's spunk and gusto. Believe what you believe, follow your dream, and don't let anybody stop you—that's who Sally is."

GENDER BENDER: As former boss lady of the now defunct Spectra Fashions, Sally often resorted to dirty tricks to one up her biggest competitor in the rag trade, Forrester Creations. The mistress of disguise has even pulled several cross-dressing capers! "Sally does man drag better than anybody," Conley says. "I remember when she had her cohort, Gladys the hairdresser, who was played by Phyllis Diller. Phyllis and I were disguised as pool men, cleaning the pool at Stephanie Forrester's (Susan Flannery) house, and Sally deservedly fell in the water. That was some of the funniest stuff that was ever on television."

NAME GAMES (OR DOGGONE COINCIDENCE): Was Rose DeVille's devilish moniker perhaps inspired by the criminal Cruella De Vil from Disney's *101 Dalmatians*? "Yes, I thought that was an alias," Conley laughs. "Cruella de Vil is probably Rose's idol!"

#9: Elizabeth Hubbard

WHY WE LOVE HER: As Dr. Althea Gibson on *The Doctors*, Elizabeth Hubbard won the very first Daytime Emmy for best actress in 1974. But she is best known as Oakdale's resident "boss lady" Lucinda Walsh. This ballsy broad—who was born Mary Ellen Walters in Peoria, Illinois—changed her name to the more diva-esque "Lucinda" and rose to riches as a powerful businesswoman. "Gay guys want to play Lucinda, you *know* they do!" Hubbard says with a laugh. "Her acquisition of wealth has given her the position to say whatever she wants to say. But she has never lost her sense of what the struggle of life is. She is embattled, not entitled. She has to fight for every damn thing. Wanting love is important to Lucinda, as a child who was kicked out and abandoned by her family. If she's been any kind of a role model, I am deeply grateful."

A GAY'S GREATEST GRANDMA: In a progressive plotline, Lucinda's teenage grandson, Luke—played by Van Hansis—recently came out of the closet. Would she ever go all homophobic and reject the kid? "Oh absolutely not!" Hubbard insists. "They better not write that because I won't do it. I won't." Fortunately, Lucinda—who took the revelation of Luke's sexual orientation in stride—seems more likely to join the Oakdale chapter of PFLAG. Heck, the corporate raider might even take over as their president!

THINGS THAT MAKE YOU GO "HUH?": "They once let me play my own mother," Hubbard recalls, rolling her eyes. "They didn't work on [the flashbacks] very hard. It was a terrible set and I had a terrible black wig on!" Another time, she recalls, "Gypsies were poisoning Lucinda by giving her these huge, smelly green drinks full of LSD. The [producers] didn't like me holding my nose to down them. I just couldn't take it seriously! They eventually dropped the whole story."

MAMA DRAMA: Although, Lucinda is now close to both her children, it wasn't always that way! Lucinda's spiteful ex-husband, Jacobo, who ruled the fictional nation of Montega, kept her away from their daughter, Sierra, until she was an adult. Lucinda also spent years clashing with adopted daughter Lily over her supercouplehood with stable boy Holden Snyder. A frustrated Lily even sued to have her own adoption nullified! Fortunately, the ungrateful little bitch got over herself and stopped short of breaking her mother's heart.

#8: Anne Heche

WHY WE LOVE HER: Long before Anne Heche's 2001 book, *Call Me Crazy*, announced that she had an alter ego called "Celestia," the actress played a dramatic dual role on the NBC soap *Another World*. From 1987-91, Heche played shy, sweet-natured heiress Marley Love and her long lost twin sister, Vicky, a bitchy, scheming slut with major abandonment issues. Here's a scandalous trivia tidbit: Marley, Vicky, and their MILFy mother, Donna Love (Anna Stuart), all slept with the same Bay City bad boy, Jake McKinnon (Tom Eplin). At the end of her *AW* run in 1991, Heche collected a Daytime Emmy trophy for outstanding younger actress in a drama series. If you missed her sudsy adventures the first time around, she's still sizzling in daily *AW* re-runs on SOAPnet.

HER HOMO HISTORY: Heche's closeted gay father Don died of AIDS in 1983. He was just 45. "I put a very high premium on honesty," Heche said in *Cosmopolitan*'s May 1997 issue. "What I learned from [my father's] death is that if you don't accept your sexuality, it will kill you." From 1997-2000, Heche was the girlfriend of out and proud comedienne Ellen DeGeneres. They were Hollywood's lesbian "It" couple until Heche left DeGeneres for Coleman "Coley" Laffoon, a cameraman who was shooting a documentary about the funny lady. DeGeneres suffered a very public heartbreak when her ex married Laffoon in 2001 and bore his son, Homer Heche Laffoon, the following year.

LIFE AFTER SOAPS: Heche is one of the most successful soap alums ever. Her primetime TV credits include memorable stints on *Ally McBeal, Everwood,* and *Nip/Tuck*. Heche's long list of film credits includes roles in *Donnie Brasco, Six Days Seven Nights, Psycho,* and *John Q.*

#7: Finola Hughes

WHY WE LOVE HER: London native Finola Hughes first grabbed America's attention in 1983's *Staying Alive*, the guilty-pleasure sequel to *Saturday Night Fever*. She played Laura, the bitchy Broadway dancer who had a torrid sexual fling with John Travolta's Tony Manero. Her character had the movie's best line, when Laura cruelly dismissed Tony after having her way with him: "We met. I liked you. We made it. What did you think it was? True love? Everybody uses everybody!" Hughes went on to join *General Hospital* in 1985 as Anna Devane, who juggled her roles as a wife and mom, with her career as a crime-fighting super spy. While battling evil,

Anna romanced dreamy dudes like Robert Scorpio (Tristan Rogers) and Duke Lavery (Ian Buchanan), and also nurtured her daughter, Robin (Kimberly McCullough), who grew up to be a doctor. In the process, Anna became one of the most popular and beloved characters in *GH* history. In May 2006, the actress reprised the role after fourteen years away from the show. A weeklong visit turned into a much longer return stint. "The response to Finola's return as Anna Devane has been very, very strong, which is wonderful," *GH* head writer Robert Guza, Jr., said at the time. "She's a capable, competent woman who can kick a man's ass, yet she's a sexy seductress *and* she's Robin's mom, having to deal with a grown daughter who's having relationship problems. Finola juggles those three aspects extremely well."

SHE LOVES HER GAYS: "The friendship between a straight woman and gay people—men and women—is the most amazing relationship, for sure. I'm being totally honest when I say that I don't think I would have a nice-sized address book if it wasn't for my gay friends. I'm not lying here. They've been incredible friends to me. They've watched my back, made sure my pantyhose was on straight, and I love 'em."

The Fairy Facts About Finola

IN 1991, FINOLA WAS MIA when her name was called during the Daytime Emmy Awards at New York's Radio City Music Hall. The winner for outstanding lead actress was stuck in the U.K. dealing with bureaucratic red tape to get her visa renewed!

DURING A COMPLICATED CROSSOVER STUNT on ABC's *All My Children* that lasted from 1999 to 2003, Finola starred as both Anna Devane (her GH character) and Anna's long-lost twin sister, Alex Devane. Confused? You're not alone, honey.

FINOLA AND DIGBY DIEHL CO-WROTE the hilariously clever novel *Soapsuds*, a thinly veiled send up of her real-life work experiences in the wacky world of daytime TV. Soap-fan speculation still abounds about that nasty "Regina Contini" character. Now just who might she be based on? "We needed that kind of a diva in order to have conflict in the book," Finola says. "The characters are just composites of people that I've met over the years. There are lots of women—and men!—on soaps who are similar to Regina. It's really not based on one person." Uh huh. If you say so, Fin.

FINOLA FREQUENTLY HAUNTED WB's witchcraft drama, *Charmed*, as the gorgeous ghost of Patty Halliwell. Patty was the much-missed mother of sister sorceresses Prue (Shannen Doherty), Piper (Holly Marie Combs), Phoebe (Alyssa Milano) and Paige (Rose McGowan). It made perfect sense that Patty had been a witch in life—she'd need magical powers to keep such a slim figure after giving birth to four daughters!

IN THE '90S, Finola played *Beaches* star Mayim Bialik's stepmother in the fifth and final season of the NBC sitcom *Blossom*.

FINOLA IS A TV FASHIONISTA who hosts the Style network's makeover show *How Do I Look?* FYI, the raven-haired looker owes her exotic beauty to a mixture of Irish and Italian roots.

IN WHAT WAS PERHAPS THE WEIRDEST moment of her career, Finola hosted the Fox reality TV special *Who's Your Daddy?* in 2005. It featured B-movie bimbo T. J. Myers (*Seduction of Innocence*) trying to sort out her biological father from a pool of eight candidates. Girls and gays everywhere were riveted by the drama—although we *did* feel a bit dirty afterward.

#6: Heather Tom

WHY WE LOVE HER: Heather Tom won two Daytime Emmy Awards during her thirteen years as sassy heiress Victoria Newman on *The Young and the Restless*. Later, she went over to *One Life to Live*, where she earned her tenth Daytime Emmy nomination as Kelly Cramer Buchanan. In fact, she holds the record for the most Daytime Emmy nominations by a performer under the age of thirty! In addition to all those accolades, Tom has officially won the hearts of her gay fans with her activism on behalf of children, women, LGBT folks, and people with AIDS. "I'm a gay man trapped in a woman's body," she laughs. "All my friends are gay. They love me because I've been really active in the community and I have great shoes! But seriously, I believe in personal freedom. It's what we as Americans are most proud of. When our basic rights are threatened or when they're not extended to *everyone*, then you really have to pay attention to that."

JUST CALL ME DIVA: "Diva is a four-letter word, but that's OK," Tom cracks. "I've grown up with some of the best daytime divas ever. Or divas, period—I don't even have to qualify it. I've learned from the best. So I'm honored to be in that category after sixteen years on daytime TV."

Heather's Heavenly Soap Facts

HEATHER'S HOT YOUNGER BROTHER, David Tom, played her half brother, Paul Cramer, on ABC's *One Life to Live*. The bad boy stole another woman's baby for her fertility-challenged character, Kelly. David also played Billy Abbott on *The Young and the Restless* while Heather was there, although their characters on the CBS sudser barely interacted with one another.

VICTORIA NEWMAN, Heather's horny heiress on *The Young and the Restless*, sure enjoyed rolling in the hay. In fact, Vicky lived in a tack house in the Newman Ranch stables, where she saddled up and rode many young stallions over the years!

HEATHER'S SISTER, Nicholle Tom, played one of Fran Drescher's young charges on *The Nanny*. Nicholle also played the kid sis of Scott Scanlon on *Beverly Hills, 90210*.

#5: Emma Samms

WHY WE LOVE HER: London lass Emma Samms joined *General Hospital* in 1982 as sophisticated con artist Holly Sutton. She was the first seriously viable love interest for Anthony Geary's Luke after

Genie Francis left the ABC soap, derailing the Luke and Laura phenomenon that had literally captivated America and carried *GH* from the brink of cancellation to No. 1 soap status. Holly was the third point of a popular love triangle between Luke and his longtime "frenemy," Robert Scorpio, as played by Aussie bad boy Tristan Rogers. Later, Samms went off to do *Dynasty* (and its spin-off, *The Colbys*), starring as the Fallon Carrington recast who made us ask "Pamela Sue Martin who?" Like many great divas, she credits the gays with her longevity. "Those are my people," Samms grins. "Absolutely, yes! They totally embraced all of *Dynasty*, but they've been very enthusiastic about me, as I have been about them!"

YOU BETTER WORK, SUPERMODELS: In the '90s, Samms starred on the too short-lived *Melrose Place* spin-off, *Models Inc.*, as modeling-agency mogul Grayson Louder. The main attraction of Aaron Spelling's fabulously awful nighttime sudser was Samms's fabulously over-the-top outfits. It was not unusual to see this bitch on heels sashay into scenes wearing cashmere and thigh-high hooker boots. "Loved those boots!" Samms says. "Nolan Miller, who designed *Dynasty*'s costumes, made all those beautiful clothes on *Models, Inc.* specially for me. In fact, that was one of my conditions when I talked to Aaron about doing the show. I said, 'Is Nolan doing the clothes?' And Aaron said, 'Well, no, but if you want, he could do yours.' So he just did mine!" Now *that's* how a diva does it.

DAYTIME COMEBACK: In 2006, Samms reprised her role

as Holly on *GH* after thirteen years away. "I had two weeks of knowing I was coming back to the show," she has said, "which is enough for me to hit the gym, but not enough time to have the major surgical repairs one would hope for." Spoken like a true soap diva.

#4: Linda Dano

WHY WE LOVE HER: Linda Dano is best known for starring on NBC's late, great *Another World* as Felicia Gallant, née Fanny Grady. (Gotta love those names.) Bay City's resident glamourpuss novelist was famous for sitting at her typewriter—um, this was back in the '80s—wrapped in a feather boa while churning out hot-blooded novels like her *Harlequin* romance, *Dreamweaver*. That's so gay I "harlecan" stand it! Felicia had a drag queen's sensibility with regard to makeup and wardrobe. When it came to eye shadow, lipstick, and clothes, nothing was ever too much. Rather than let Felicia's big hats and shoulder pads wear her, though, Dano pulled off over-the-top looks flawlessly, always stealing scenes from co-stars with her huge heart and inimitable style.

WHAT A DOLL: AW scribe Robert Soderberg based the Felicia character on Jacqueline Susann, the '70s celebutante author of *Valley of the Dolls*, who was later played by Bette "The Divine Miss M" Midler in the big-screen biopic *Isn't She Great*. It doesn't get any gayer than all that, kids.

THINGS THAT MAKE YOU GO "HUH": In a soapy rip-off of

Stephen King's *Misery*, Walter Trask, an obsessed reader vexed that she'd quit writing romances to focus on her memoirs, held Felicia captive. Locking Felicia in an attic with a sturdy combination lock on the door, Walter demanded she pen another bodice-ripper just for him. Worse yet, he forced Ms. Gallant to dine with him in a period gown that resembled a giant lace doily, and drink champagne, despite her dedication to sobriety as an AA member. Hey, at least he didn't bust her ankles like Kathy Bates did to James Caan in the movie! A soap diva should never be humbled by getting "hobbled." How would she ever wear high heels again?

CELEBRITY SERENADE: Think you're Linda Dano's feyest fan? Sorry, but that credit must go to the legendary Liberace. "He invited me to the opening of his show at Radio City Music Hall," Dano recalls. "That's how I knew he was a fan. We first met backstage there." Shortly before his death in the mid-eighties, the famously flamboyant pianist made two guest appearances on *AW* at his gal pal Dano's invitation. Once, Liberace's outfit nearly upstaged the bride's when he performed at Felicia's wedding to Zane Lindquist, the third of her four husbands. Another time, he sang "I'll Be Seeing You" to Felicia in his very own Trump Tower *pied-à-terre*. "He was making little food treats for all the *Another World* crew at four in the morning," Dano recalls. "What a lovely, lovely man. When he died, I received a gift from him. It was a cut crystal star from Baccarat. It was magnificent and I treasure it. And now I know he's one of my angels that looks out for me. Lee and my husband [the late Frank Attardi] are great friends in heaven."

RAY OF LIGHT: After *AW*'s cancellation, Dano made daytime history as Dr. Rae Cummings, a character who crossed over on four ABC soaps: *All My Children, General Hospital, One Life to Live*, and *Port Charles*. Although Rae started out as a respected therapist, Dano soon tired of playing a one-dimensional lady doc who just listened to other peoples' troubles. So *OLTL* cleverly exposed Rae as an unqualified quack who had actually stolen her diploma from a guy named Dr. *Ray* Cummings!

#3: Robin Strasser

WHY WE LOVE HER: Robin Strasser is best known as Llanview's resident bitch, Dorian Cramer Lord, on *One Life to Live*. It's a role she has played with divalicious gusto on and off since 1979.

VIKI AND DORIAN: REAL LIFE RIVALS? The entrepreneurial Dorian Lord has had many unseemly careers—disgraced doctor, scandal-rag editrix, black widow—as well as six husbands and many more lovers. She is mistress of a grand house called La Boulaie, which is French for "birch tree plantation." Dorian also has two daughters, Cassie and Adriana, both of whom were raised elsewhere and turned up on her doorstep as angst-ridden young adults. Oddly, the one constant in Dorian's life is her arch nemesis Victoria "Viki" Lord (Erika Slezak), the eldest daughter of her wealthy, perversely evil first husband, Victor. Like many stepparents and stepchildren, Dorian and Viki hated each other from day one—and it's stayed that way for decades. These two are sometimes jokingly referred to as a soap "supercouple" because they have one of daytime's greatest long-running feuds. It seems Dorian simply can't mind her own business and quit messing with Viki! Stepmommie Dearest has found ways to annoy literally *all* of the troubled Viki's multiple personalities over the years. "Dorian *thinks* she's living her own life," Strasser laughs. "She thinks she's doing a great job. It's just that this other woman keeps intruding!" Unlike their alter egos on the screen, Strasser insists she and Erika Slezak aren't foes, just excellent sparring partners at the *One Life* studio. "Good divas work beautifully together," she says. "My definition of an evil diva is somebody who thinks they have to be center stage in the spotlight and diminish the other people around them in order to be the star. That is *not* a good diva. The good leading lady works well with other divas on the same stage. It just raises the bar. You're telling me Erika Slezak isn't major? You can't argue with six Emmys. I'm never *not* scared to death when I walk on set with her. She has an astounding memory, range . . . she almost never makes a mistake! I'm always panting to keep up, and I work much harder on learning the lines ahead of time. I go out ready for anything. Complacency is not a good word to me."

Robin's Roles of a Lifetime

ALTHOUGH DORIAN CRAMER LORD is her signature role,

Robin Strasser has happily had more than *One Life to Live* in the daytime suds.

ANOTHER WORLD: Before Victoria Wyndham began her twenty-five-year reign in Bay City as Rachel Davis, Robin Strasser originated the role in 1967. Agnes Nixon created Rachel as a classic soap-opera archetype: The stunningly beautiful brunette from lower-class origins who's obsessed with stealing a hot, rich preppie from his angelic blonde girlfriend. "I didn't even know I was pretty then," Strasser muses. "I honestly had no idea until I looked back on photographs years later."

ALL MY CHILDREN: Strasser spent 1976–79 in Pine Valley as a much lusted-after lady doctor, Christina Karras. In one strange plotline, Christina was revealed to be a self-hating psychotic who unknowingly sent herself hate letters and death threats. Yikes! "Doctor, heal thyself, honey."

KNOTS LANDING: OK, this one's not a daytime soap, but it must be mentioned that back in 1989-90, *Knots* fans loved to hate Strasser as Dianne Kirkwood. Dianne was a ruthless TV producer who was suspected of stalking talk show host Karen McKenzie, as played by Michele Lee. Things got ugly when Karen received a bouquet of flowers containing live snakes. Turned out, Dianne wasn't the real stalker, but she was guilty of doing her damndest to steal Karen's gig as host of the chat fest, "Open Mike."

PASSIONS: Strasser did a super-kooky stint from 2001–02 as Hecuba, the deliciously diabolical rival of Harmony's resident 300-year-old witch, Tabitha Lenox (Juliet Mills). Hecuba's many evil achievements include: stealing a teenage slut's soul and wearing it around her neck in a glowing purple vial; hostessing a Chinese-food restaurant called Hecuba's Hunan Hell; and trapping good witch Charity Standish (Molly Stanton) inside a walk-in closet, which was really a flaming portal into Hell itself. (And us gays thought we had closet issues?!) Every time Hecuba declared, "Hell is ready for you, Charity!" fans cheered her on in spite of ourselves. In one of *the* campiest soap-opera moments of all time, Hecuba did a satanic disco dance outside Charity's closet to The Trammps's 1977 hit "Disco Inferno." Burn baby burn! "I'm a not-so-closeted comedian," Strasser admits with a chuckle. "I was thrilled when *Passions*'s executive producer Lisa Hesser called and said, 'Would you consider coming on and playing a witch?' I said, 'Halloween for a paycheck? Definitely!' I had a lot of fun, but I also enjoyed the show's style and humor. I can't understand why they're always snubbed at the Daytime Emmys, because they deserve accolades. You do *not* compare *Passions* to the other soap operas. It's its own baby. It's a cult classic in the making, just like *Dark Shadows* and *Mary Hartman, Mary Hartman*."

#2: Jeanne Cooper

WHY WE LOVE HER: Hollywood veteran Jeanne Cooper has been a series regular on *The Young and the Restless* since the CBS sudser debuted in 1973. She plays Katherine "Kay" Chancellor, the grande dame of high society in Genoa City, Wisconsin.

INSIDE SCOOP: SSSH! CENSORING THE L WORD

Back in 1976, *Y&R* flirted with same-sex attraction when the lonely Kay welcomed her gal pal Joann Curtis (Kay Heberle) as a houseguest in her manse. You see, Kay was between stable boys and Joann was a neglected housewife, whose cheating hubby lacked appreciation for her plus-sized figure. "Joann was fat," Cooper recalls candidly. "Through Katherine helping her start losing weight, an admiration began. It was meant to be very sweet. It wasn't a sexual preference thing. Most women, if they are honest with themselves, will admit there's at least a period in one's life where you feel more comfortable with a woman than with a man because you are at a resting place. With men, you have to compromise, give in, be hurt, and repair your soul. There's just no pressure to do or be anything with another woman. She listens and understands."

While Kay and Joann were never overtly romantic, the mere hint of lesbianism was enough to incite homophobic fan mail and hurt *Y&R*'s ratings. "We were getting ready to go on a cruise to Hawaii together," Cooper recalls. "In fact, I think I put my hand on her shoulder and she put her hand over mine, which was acceptable. I mean we didn't see anything wrong with that. But boy, I'll tell you, for people whose minds are pure, the Bible Belt really picked up on *that* fast!

"This story was intelligently constructed, poetically done, well written," she adds. "The gay awakening was happening in the '70s and we thought it would be a great story line. But no matter how gently you approached homosexuality at that time, it was totally unacceptable because all people could see was the sex angle. 'How do they have sex?' That is what absolutely killed it. What a shame. These Bible Belt viewers couldn't see the need of having somebody to talk to and be close with?"

"This is a woman of power and style who gets her brains beaten in occasionally in love affairs, but she survives," Cooper says. "I have a tremendous gay fan base because Katherine is a survivor. If they were going to be a woman, she's who they would want to be!"

STAMP OF APPROVAL: British actor Terence Stamp has said that *Y&R*'s Katherine inspired his dignified portrayal of Bernadette, a transgender Aussie drag artist, in 1994's hit comedy, *The Adventures of Priscilla, Queen of the Desert*. "It was amazing that he'd studied the shows I had done," Cooper marvels. "What a great compliment."

LOVE THY ENEMY: "I Love to Hate You" isn't just the title of an Erasure song, kids. It's the lifelong motto of soap-opera rivals who share decades of deep, mutual loathing, yet can't stay away from each other. Since the '70s, *Y&R* fans have considered Katherine Chancellor and Jill Foster Abbott a supercouple because of their endlessly entertaining feud. The sluttish Jill—who's been played at various times by Bond Gideon, Brenda Dickson, Melinda O. Fee, and Jess Walton—stole Kay's husband, Phillip Chancellor. After a complex legal dispute over the zillionaire's estate, both wife and mistress ended up living in his mansion together! "Don't forget that Jill was originally Katherine's manicurist and *paid companion*," Cooper winks. "You want a story that is a very strange one? These two women . . . Please! There's a relationship that has to explain itself even to this day." (FYI, Kay literally had a stroke in 2003 when Jill was revealed to be the bastard daughter she'd given up for adoption.)

#1: Susan Lucci

WHY WE LOVE HER: Susan Lucci is a sexy, sassy superstar who truly needs no introduction. But here's one anyway! Ever since *All My Children* debuted on ABC in 1970, she has played Erica Kane, the most famous character in the history of daytime television. Even those uninitiated folks who turn up their noses at the soaps know Lucci's name. By the 1980s, she was one of the few soap actresses who graced the covers of major magazines and appeared as a guest on top talk shows. (It was Regis Philbin who originally dubbed her "La Lucci" on *Live with Regis & Kathie Lee*, and his affectionate nickname stuck.) Throughout the 1980s and '90s, she was not only the Queen of Daytime, but also quite a movie-of-the-week maven. Some of her classic MOW titles include *Mafia Princess, Haunted by Her Past, Lady Mobster, The Woman Who Sinned, French Silk*, and *Seduced and Betrayed*. They were generally campy, fun edge-of-your-seat thrillers starring Lucci as the dangerous seductress—and we ate 'em up! What really made La Lucci a household name was her seemingly endless string of losses at the Daytime Emmy Awards. This versatile, hard-working leading lady was nominated a whopping eighteen times—the first nod was in 1978—without winning. In 1999, Lucci got her nineteenth nomination and snagged the outstanding lead actress trophy at last. She received an unprecedented four-minute standing ovation. (The author of this book, who was watching from home, projectile cried so hard that his tears actually hit the TV screen!) In the years since Lucci's victory, the Nielsen ratings for the Daytime Emmy Awards have been in steady decline—some experts blame the lack of annual "Will Susan Lucci *finally* win or won't she?" suspense. It has become a very common pop culture reference to say that any celebrity repeatedly snubbed at an awards show "pulled a Susan Lucci." Still, the loyal fans who've followed her colorful career throughout the years know that there is only *one* La Lucci.

Fabulous Facts About Susan Lucci

HER CHARACTER, ERICA KANE, has been married eleven times to a total of nine husbands. She married two of them twice! One of those two-time spouses was Dimitri Marrick, who was played by *Dynasty* star Michael Nader. The tall, dark, and handsome actor also portrayed her Mafioso love interest in *Lady Mobster*.

LUCCI HAS BEEN MARRIED to Helmut Huber since 1969. They share two children, Andreas and Liza. Having followed in her mom's soap-acting footsteps, Liza is an original cast member of NBC's *Passions*, where she plays Gwen Hotchkiss Winthrop.

1990 WAS AN *ANNUS FABULOUS* for Lucci, who hosted NBC's *Saturday Night Live* and began a yearlong stint on *Dallas* as the devious Hillary Taylor (aka Sheila Foley).

LUCCI REALIZED HER DREAM of starring on Broadway when she took over the lead role from Bernadette Peters in a revival of *Annie Get Your Gun* from 1999-2000.

AMONG ERICA KANE'S MANY glamorous jobs on *AMC* was CEO of Enchantment Cosmetics. Life imitates art for Lucci, who has made millions as a celebrity endorser of perfumes, makeup, skin, and haircare products.

FOR YEARS, LUCCI HAS BEEN pestered by fanciful rumors that she is the secret daughter of comedienne Phyllis Diller and/or the sister of *One Life to Live* diva Robin Strasser. She is not related to either of these ladies, fabulous though they may be.

GIRLS ON THE SIDE

THESE DELICIOUS DIVAS ALSO DESERVE HONORABLE MENTIONS FOR BEING BOTH BOLD AND BEAUTIFUL.

ALISON SWEENEY, *DAYS OF OUR LIVES*: Sweeney is a big fan fave as Salem's sassified queen of schemes, Samantha "Sami" Brady. Sami is nothing like her saintly, long-suffering mother, Dr. Marlena Evans (Deidre Hall). Girlfriend concocts ways to make *others* suffer, but it's all in the name of finding the true love she lacks. "Sami *definitely* has a lot of gay fans," Sweeney says. "It's always funny when guys come up and ask me what it's like to make out with my co-stars, Austin Peck and Bryan Dattilo!"

KATHERINE KELLY LANG, *THE BOLD AND THE BEAUTIFUL*: As lovelorn Los Angeles fashionista Brooke Logan Forrester, she has slept her way through the Forrester family and even bedded her own daughter's husband. Somehow, though, Lang always gets us to sympathize with the slutty Brooke. The fact that she's played this meaty role since 1987 and *never* been nominated for a Daytime Emmy is shameful. "That's very nice of you!" Lang says. "As long as I go to work and I drive home feeling good about what I did that day, that's good enough for me."

ILENE KRISTEN, *ONE LIFE TO LIVE*: The Brooklyn-born Kristen rose to soap stardom as the scrappy Delia Coleridge on *Ryan's Hope* in the 1970s and '80s. These days, she adds much-needed comic relief to *One Life*'s Llanview as malaprop-dropping hairdresser Roxy Balsom. "Way back when Roxy had hypoglycemia," the actress recalls, "I came up with almost every weird [mispronunciation, like] 'hypoglucosamine,' 'hypoglaucoma,' 'hypoguacamole'. I did 'em all!"

EILEEN FULTON, *AS THE WORLD TURNS*: Fulton has been living it up in Oakdale as mouthy, much-married troublemaker Lisa Miller since 1960. Well, except for a brief detour in 1965 to headline Lisa's very own primetime spin-off serial, *Our Private World*.

LINDSAY KORMAN HARTLEY, *PASSIONS*: When *Passions* debuted in 1999, we met Theresa Lopez-Fitzgerald, the sharp-tongued housekeeper's daughter who never stops plotting to land the preppie lad she loves, Ethan Winthrop, who's been played by hotties Travis Schuldt and Eric Martsolf. When Hartley's big brown eyes well up with those splendid soap-opera tears, she makes us forget all Theresa's desperate deeds—even that time she signed over her soul to the Devil!

Q

Soap Divas

1. Which of these Hollywood divas named Joan has never appeared on a daytime soap?

   a. *Joan Crawford*
   b. *Joan Collins*
   c. *Joan Van Ark*
   d. *Joan Fontaine*
   e. *Joan Allen*

2. Who has played Dorian Lord on *One Life to Live* the longest?

   a. *Nancy Pinkerton*
   b. *Robin Strasser*
   c. *Claire Malis*
   d. *Elaine Princi*

3. How many characters has Genie Francis played on the daytime soaps?

   a. *1*
   b. *2*
   c. *3*
   d. *4*

Soap Divas

4. Which sexy Hollywood blonde starred as Sydney Chase on ABC's short-lived daytime sudser *The City*?

   a. *Donna Mills*
   b. *Bo Derek*
   c. *Pamela Anderson*
   d. *Loni Anderson*
   e. *Morgan Fairchild*

5. Which soap-opera veteran has won the most Daytime Emmy Awards for outstanding lead actress?

   a. *Erika Slezak*
   b. *Kim Zimmer*
   c. *Susan Flannery*
   d. *Susan Lucci*
   e. *Eileen Fulton*

Lisa Rinna

WE SUDS FANS love our Lisa Rinna for so many reasons. Her famously full, sensuous lips helped make her a sex symbol on NBC's *Days of our Lives*, where she played bad girl Billie Holliday Reed from 1992–95 and again in 2002–03. Billie was an ex-junkie and porn star who relentlessly schemed to break up Salem supercouple Hope and Bo Brady. Rinna was also hilariously funny as *Melrose Place*'s trashiest troublemaker, Taylor McBride. Later on, she went on to co-host SOAPnet's chatfest, *Soap Talk*, with *One Life to Live* stud Ty Treadway. During the chatfest's four seasons, the bubbly, scxy duo, shared three Daytime Emmy nominations for outstanding talk show host.

[COURTESY E. J. CAMP FOR SOAPnet]

Lisa Rinna

Rinna tasted primetime success again in 2006 as a highly popular finalist on ABC's hit celebrity hoofing contest, *Dancing with the Stars*. Here, the busy soap diva pauses for a moment to share her warm 'n' fuzzy feelings for Lisa aficionados.

Caught your recent shout out to your gay fans on Soap Talk. *Very cool!*
I must've been a gay man in a past life. Some of my best friends are gay. I have my girlfriends and there's a certain kind of intimacy with a girlfriend, but I connect on a deeper level with a gay man than I do with a girlfriend.

What are the gays like when they talk to you?
They're some of the nicest fans ever. I just think the gay community is so awesome. I have such reverence. I really do. It's no accident that my husband, Harry Hamlin, did one of the first gay movies, *Making Love*, in 1982. We have a special place in our hearts for you all.

Why do you think we gravitate so much toward your kooky characters, like Taylor on Melrose Place?
Well, I'm always playing crazy or I'm a big bitch! They also like my style. It has to do with the fashion element, I think.

Your edgy look is just on the border of OTT—over the top—but hot.

Yeah! I had a guy come up to me in Barneys the other day and he told me he had a haircut like mine. [*Laughs*] His hair looked way better than mine, and he was fabulous. It was just so cute. I love that. My fan base, they just love a great diva. They love somebody who's not afraid of fashion or showing off. They love someone who's fearless.

Your camptastic antics were definitely the best part of Melrose Place's latter years.

I think the two years I was on were really good and the gays loved Taylor McBride 'cause she's OTT. The shorter my outfit was, the weirder I was. The crazier I was, the more scandalous or slutty I was, the better. They loved it!

NANNY AND THE PROFESSOR STAR JULIET MILLS
NOW CASTS A DAILY SPELL ON THE TROUBLED TOWN
OF HARMONY AS THE WITCHY "TABITHA," ON NBC'S
PASSIONS. (COURTESY OF NBC UNIVERSAL)

Ooh, Ooh Witchy Women of Daytime

"She is almost a drag character."

PLENTY OF soap-opera scheme queens are just witches with a capital B. But a few of them are actually bona fide broom-riding, cauldron-stirring, crystal-ball-gazing witches! This chapter conjures forth an unholy trinity of sorceresses who have cast their camptastic spells on soap fans over the years. These formidable ladies know how to hurl a curse without using four-letter words.

Juliet Mills

WHY WE LOVE HER: Although British actress Juliet Mills started out on stage and in films, she really found fame in America as the star of ABC's *Nanny and the Professor*. In the endearing *Mary Poppins*–ish '70s TV series, she played a psychic babysitter named Nanny Phoebe Figalilly. She was also demonically possessed Exorcist-style in the 1974 horror flick

Chi Sei? Then in 1975, Mills played a victim of possession again in the TV movie *Demon, Demon*. Oh, and she later appeared in 1992's spooky *Waxwork II: Lost in Time*. Anyone notice a career trend here?

Mills's witchy resume made her perfect casting for James E. Reilly's outrageous supernatural soap, *Passions*. Since 1999, she has played Tabitha Lenox, the 300-year-old witch who wreaks havoc in a coastal New England hamlet, ironically called Harmony. Reilly's scripts include frequent references to his favorite classic sitcom, *Bewitched*; he not only dubbed Mills's character Tabitha, but gave her a very late-in-life baby daughter named Endora!

"You can't get more camp than that," Mills laughs. "It's pretty blatant! Tabitha's not that different from Nanny Phoebe Figalilly. I was always talking to dogs, cats, and chickens. And now I'm talking to dolls and babies. I know *Passions* appeals to gays and, of course, naturally my character would. Because I'm a fag hag, aren't I? Tabitha is and I am, too, sometimes. I suppose most of the stuff I'm involved in is high camp. I like going to gay bars, gay discos, gay *everything*!

"I've also always been very popular with the gay guys because I married Maxwell Caulfield [of *Grease 2* and *The Colbys* fame], so that was a good start. Maxwell always has had a huge gay following."

Speaking of Juliet's fabulous family relations, she is the daughter of the late actor Sir John Mills and the sister of *The Parent Trap*'s Hayley Mills. Her

godfather was the late, gay playwright Noel Coward
and her godmother was the late Hollywood icon
Vivien Leigh, who played Scarlett O'Hara in *Gone
with the Wind.*

Tribute:

FRIENDS FOREVER: Before Tabby's baby came along, her
beloved sidekick and confidante was Timmy, a
living rag doll played by 3-foot-2-inch actor Josh
Ryan Evans. Like Pinocchio, Timmy wished to
become a human boy and eventually did. Although
Evans was an adult, he had the appearance and
voice of a child due to achondroplasia, a form
of dwarfism. On August 5, 2002, Evans died of a
congenital heart condition at the age of twenty. In
an eerie parallel, Timmy *also* died of heart failure in
the hospital on that very day's episode of *Passions.*
The soap had planned to kill off the Timmy
character and resurrect him after a brief period.
"Josh's death came as a complete surprise to all of
us," *Passions*'s executive producer Lisa Hesser said
at the time. "We were aware that Josh had a heart
condition, however his hiatus from the show was
purely storyline driven. We had every intention of
bringing the character back to the show."

The quirky combo of the witch and her talking
doll put *Passions* on the TV map in its early years,
helping the fledgling soap achieve the kind of
mainstream notoriety only previously enjoyed
only by soap icons like Susan Lucci and *General
Hospital*'s Luke and Laura. "I feel Josh's presence in
some ways," Juliet Mills says. "I'm still working on

the very same set we worked on for three years. He was very much a believer in spirits, angels, fairies and all of that, and I believe in all of that, too. So I'm sure he's around."

Robin Strasser

SHE PLAYED HECUBA, a witch to rival Harmony's resident sorceress, Tabitha. For more information, check out the Soap Divas chapter.

Tanya Boyd

WHY WE LOVE HER: Although her real speaking voice is quite high and girlish, Tanya Boyd puts on a deep French accent to play Celeste Perrault on NBC's *Days of our Lives*. Back in 1994, Celeste was introduced as the psychic sidekick of Salem supervillain Stefano DiMera (Joseph Mascolo), although she was ultimately reformed. She frequently speaks *Franglais*, exclaiming dramatic things like "Oh no! *Mon dieu!*" when her tarot cards reveal ominous signs and portents; which they usually do. Nobody can stay happy for too long on *Days*.

DRAG DAUGHTER: Although black women often enjoy dressing colorfully, Celeste goes much further than most. Since she is a lover of big hats and flashy wigs, the color and length of her hair changes weekly! "Our costume designer, Richard Bloore, has been Daytime Emmy nominated, and he's a fabulous shopper," Boyd smiles. "He knows Celeste pretty well . . . She is almost a drag character. That's what

I love about drag queens, to be honest with you. They are not afraid to take fashion to the extreme. That's what the public wants to see! Many gay guys and drag queens watch *Days* and they tell me, 'Girl, you are it!' And I love that because I love people. It doesn't matter what your thing is. As long as you're a good person, that's all I care about.

"I learn a lot from gay guys who dress up and do drag shows," Boyd adds enthusiastically. "In fact, when I was a little girl in Detroit, there was a female impersonator that lived in my building. I was always at his apartment watching him do his makeup and hair. I always liked that flamboyancy. Subconsciously, that might be where I get a lot of that from 'cause he was fabulous!"

SALEM SECRETS: Dr. Alexandra "Lexie" Carver was recently revealed to be the secret mixed-race love child of Celeste and the evil Stefano. "My daughter is very wealthy because Stefano gave her plenty of money and jewels," Boyd says in character. "We hid those jewels in a wall, but I haven't forgotten about those jewels, believe me. If times get hard, I *will* be tapping on the wall! Pull out a little diamond here, a little ruby there . . . it's all good."

OOH, OOH, WITCHY WOMAN: Tanya Boyd and Celeste share a strong faith in the occult. "I feel James E. Reilly, who is the [former] head writer of both *Days*, really does have a deep spiritual sensibility," she says. "When I first got this job, I thought, 'How great to get paid to play something on television that I really believe in!' I am into reading tarot cards. I had a great aunt who was very psychic. We just didn't have Celeste's crystals that move around all by themselves! I do feel glad that Jim keeps her using her powers for the good side, though. I don't want any demons getting ideas about *me*!"

Lara Parker

WHY WE LOVE HER: Long before American soap viewers were introduced to Susan Lucci as *All My Children*'s Erica Kane or Joan Collins as *Dynasty*'s Alexis Carrington, there was Lara Parker. The blonde barracuda was a masterful practitioner of witchcraft and bitchcraft as Angelique DuVall Collins on *Dark Shadows*. During the supernatural sudser's five-year run on ABC from 1966-71, teens rushed home from school to watch the lovelorn witch raise unholy hell at Collinwood.

"The bitch you love to hate was a concept that had been done in '30s films with Joan Crawford and Bette Davis, but not much on goody-goody television in those days," Parker says. "There were a lot of troubled teenagers who especially liked Angelique because she was smart, sarcastic, and she had power. She could make people suffer when they made her mad! If Angelique was ever away for awhile and she returned, it meant horrible things were going to happen to everybody."

LOVE BITES: A lowly servant girl , Angelique, cursed the blue-blooded Barnabas Collins (Jonathan Frid) to dwell in misery as a broody vampire. What was Angie's damage anyway? "Barnabas had seduced and abandoned Angelique," Parker says. "He loved

Josette DuPres (Kathryn Leigh Scott), a lady of his own class. Hell hath no fury like a woman scorned. I had lots of voodoo dolls!

"Because I always wished I could be the ingénue of the show, I played Angelique's sympathetic side, not just the evil. Since she had powers, she was not about to give up, and yet Barnabas continued to resist her. She would try very, very hard to win his love back and when she didn't succeed, she turned mean. Angelique didn't take any shit from anybody."

QUOTE ANGELIQUE'S CURSE: "I set a curse upon you, Barnabas Collins! You wanted your Josette so much? Well, you shall have her, but not in the way that you would have chosen. You will never rest, Barnabas! And you will never be able to love anyone—for whoever loves you will die. That is my curse, and you will live with it through all eternity!"

EVIL TWIN ALERT: Like other *Dark Shadows* cast members, Parker played multiple roles as the soap switched between the past and present. "For a brief time, I played Angelique and my good sister, Alexis," she recalls. "I once had a conversation with myself lying in a coffin!" At various times, Parker also played Cassandra Collins, Valerie Collins, Catherine Harridge Collins and Miranda DuVall.

IN THE 1990S, NOW MOVIE-STAR RYAN PHILLIPPE
PLAYED GAY-TEEN "BILLY DOUGLAS" ON ABC'S
ONE LIFE TO LIVE. (© STEVE FENN/AMERICAN
BROADCASTING COMPANIES, INC.)

CHAPTER SEVEN

Gay Characters on the Soaps

QUOTE

> "Backburner?!
> She was practically
> in the freezer!"

Days of our Invisible, Gay Lives

DAYTIME DRAMAS eventually gathered fans from all walks of life, including many gays and lesbians. While our scandal-loving soaps don't shy away from much, they've always been touchy about broaching the topic of homosexuality for fear of spooking the audience. To show two nice, normal guys or girls on a date together? Nah, that's just too "out there."

Hence, we GLBT viewers haven't seen too many reflections of the gay days of our lives on the soaps. Some shows barely acknowledge the existence of gays in American society. For example, *The Bold and the Beautiful* is the continuing saga of fashionistas in Los Angeles. Although both L.A. and the fashion industry are Mecca's for gays in real life, there are zero homos in this story. The *B&B* characters who toil in the rag trade, as fashion designers, are mostly guys, yet all of 'em are straight. *C'mon*! The gayest thing on the CBS sudser is the camptastic Sally Spectra, as played by raucous redhead Darlene Conley. (Read all about her in the Top 10 Soap Divas chapter.)

Just because you haven't seen openly gay characters on some soaps doesn't mean the writers haven't *tried* to introduce them, though. Back in 1977, *Another World* scribe Harding Lemay intended to have college student Michael Randolph come out to his parents, John and Pat. Lemay planned to let Michael have a boyfriend, but keep him off-screen. *AW*'s production company, Procter & Gamble, nixed that story before anything hit the screen at all.

Over on *Days of our Lives* in the mid-70s, Mike Horton thought he might be gay because he felt no physical desire for his pretty female roommate. A tryst with his father's slutty ex-girlfriend conveniently "cured" Mike of that silly notion, and he never questioned his sexual orientation afterward. This odd scenario was terribly *Tea and Sympathy* and smelled like a cop out. Speaking of gay stories that stalled, *The Young and the Restless* hinted at a lesbian attraction between socialite Katherine Chancellor (as played by the great Jeanne Cooper) and a female friend in 1975, then abandoned the story. (Read Cooper's candid recollection of Kay's abbreviated same-sex romance in the Top 10 Soap Divas chapter.)

More recently, *One Life to Live* writer Michael Malone allegedly planned to make Joey Buchanan gay. The character had been recast six times—most recently with blond hottie Bruce Michael Hall in 2003—and

OLTL had never really quite figured out what to do with Joey as a character. While a gay son's coming out story could've provided more Emmy-worthy material for Erika Slezak, who plays the ABC soap's long-suffering matriarch Victoria "Viki" Lord, *OLTL* made him an Episcopal priest instead. Talk about a Debbie Downer.

Who's Gay in Soaptown, USA?

Now that we've covered who *isn't* gay on the soaps, let's talk about who is! Here's a comprehensive soap-by-soap list of all the major (and several minor) queer characters that have appeared throughout the years. For our purposes, we'll stick to folks whose sexual orientations have been clearly established.

All My Children

QUEER CHARACTER: Dr. Lynn Carson

ACTOR: Donna Pescow (*Saturday Night Fever, Angie, Out of This World*)

THE HOMO HISTORY: In 1983, Devon Shepard McFadden (Tricia Pursley Hawkins) was rejected by Cliff Warner and turned to psychotherapist Lynn Carson for support. Soon after Lynn shared the fact that she was gay—establishing herself as daytime's first out and proud lesbian—Devon developed a girl-on-girl crush. The sensitive and sensible Lynn talked her out of it.

"We don't know that Devon was gay, other than that she was bicurious," recalls Mimi Torchin, founding editor-in-chief of *Soap Opera Weekly*.

"Devon was drawn to this woman who was warm and caring. Although Lynn did have feelings for Devon, she felt Devon wasn't gay and that she was emotionally unstable. It was responsible of Lynn not to pursue her client. They didn't even have a kiss—that would've been shocking at the time. However, it was a storyline that was still daring. *AMC* still had a lesbian character that was a good person and nobody hated her. She didn't hang herself in the attic like in *The Children's Hour*! It was fairly advanced for the time."

QUEER CHARACTER: Michael Delaney

ACTOR: Chris Bruno

THE HOMO HISTORY: Back in 1995, the faculty of Pine Valley High School included America's hottest history teacher, Michael Delaney. He was also the bravest. During a lesson about the atrocities of World War II, Mr. Delaney showed his students a poster from the U.S. Holocaust Memorial Museum. Pointing at a pink triangle, the teacher said, "This one's for me because I'm gay."

Prior to the revelation of his sexual orientation, the muscular Michael was established as an honorable ex-Marine, a caring friend to Dixie Martin (Cady McClain), and a good uncle. As a result of his classroom confession, Michael faced a hailstorm of harassment. Someone wrote, "fag," on his blackboard. Ignorant townsfolk called for his firing for fear he might somehow "teach homosexuality" to his pupils. Worst of all, his sister, Laurel Dillon, died by a bigot's bullet that was intended for him. (Keep reading for more on that.) On the bright side, Michael's brother-in-law and attorney, Trevor Dillon, successfully saved his job in a lawsuit against the Pine Valley school board. Michael also moved in with his boyfriend, Dr. Brad Phillips (Daniel McDonald). The only on-screen intimacy the guys ever shared was a bear hug, though.

In a happy ending for *AMC*, the soap earned a Daytime Emmy for Outstanding Drama Series Writing as well as an award from GLAAD (the Gay and Lesbian Alliance Against Defamation).

QUEER CHARACTER: Kevin Sheffield
ACTOR: Ben Jorgensen
THE HOMO HISTORY: In 1998, the adorable Kevin Sheffield popped up in Pine Valley as a close pal of Kelsey Jefferson (TC Warner). A sweet-natured queer teen, he looked to his openly gay teacher, Michael Delaney, for advice on coming out. Kevin was later tossed out of his family's home and invited to live in the mansion of Opal and Palmer Cortlandt, who also paid his tuition at Pine Valley University. If only all the world's disowned gay teenagers had it so good!

Things got ugly when Michael Delaney went on Pine Valley's local talk show, "The Cutting Edge," to discuss his life. Kevin's belligerent older brother, Jason, got drunk and toted a gun to the TV station with the intent to kill his brother's gay teacher. Instead, he accidentally shot and killed Michael's sister, Laurel Dillon. As if that weren't bad enough, Kevin's mother later sent him to a quack therapist who attempted to "cure" him of his homosexuality. Kevin tried playing it straight to regain his family's love, but eventually gave that up. He was last seen waiting tables at Holidays on the same day the restaurant was destroyed by an explosion. Although *AMC* has said that Kevin didn't die in the disaster, the character hasn't been seen on-screen since. Yikes!

QUEER CHARACTER: Bianca Montgomery
ACTOR: Eden Riegel
THE HOMO HISTORY: On Christmas Eve in 2000, *All My Children* made gay TV history again when Bianca, the beloved daughter of daytime's most famous diva, Erica Kane (Susan Lucci), came out to her mom as a lesbian. This was an unsettling blow to the feminine pride of Erica—a vain and self-centered celebrity who goes through husbands like Kleenex—but La Kane eventually wised up and came around.

For five years, Bianca was the center of several stories regarding her sexual orientation. In 2003, Bianca had a memorable romance with Erica's bisexual bookkeeper, Lena Kundera, who was played by the strikingly beautiful Polish actress Olga Sosnovska. Soon "Lianca"—the soap fans' fanciful amalgam for the ladies' names—were cult favorites. On Internet message boards, many gay and straight viewers alike, proved to be very involved and invested in the pure romance of "Lianca."

Tragedy struck when Bianca was raped by the evil billionaire Michael Cambias (William de Vry). This marked the beginning of the end for "Lianca." *AMC*'s honchos, who apparently lost interest in the popular lesbian coupling, contrived a shady connection between Lena and Michael, so that a "betrayed" Bianca would angrily persist in pushing her girlfriend away. Turns out, Lena was the creep's ex-lover whom Michael blackmailed into a career in corporate espionage by threatening her mother's life. "I'm not a temptress and I'm not a courtesan," Lena lamented in one episode. "I'm a whore." Viewers were sickened that Lena—a beautiful, smart lady whose love for Bianca was real—suffered so many indignities. She just couldn't catch a break!

The soap was focused on Bianca as a solo act: the long-suffering, saintly soap heroine. Bianca bravely decided to carry and keep her rapist's spawn, only to have that baby daughter, Miranda, stolen at birth. This sparked an epic baby-switch saga that involved characters crossing over between *AMC* and *One Life to Live*. It took a long time before Bianca learned that Miranda, who was presumed dead, actually was being raised by her own duplicitous best friend, Babe Chandler (Alexa Havins).

Meanwhile, Lena was oddly back burnered for an eight-month period until Olga Sosnovska's *AMC* contract finally expired. "Backburner?! She was practically in the freezer!" Mimi Torchin declares. "There would be these fabulous dramatic scenes with Lena crying against Bianca's door about once a month. Bianca shut her out of her life and Lena had no other way to express herself. She was so isolated. After one of the major rejections, Lena tried to commit suicide by taking rat poison, which was totally out of character for her.

"The show let down their viewers," Torchin adds. "They sucked us in, they did something admirable, it was accepted by the audience, and they got a ratings boost. It seemed as though they had done enough of that lesbian stuff and they wanted to move on. There was no place for 'Lianca' to go but to bed, to more intimacy, and that was the kind of relationship they didn't feel like portraying. There was definitely a bias against the Lena character and against the fact that 'Lianca' were so popular together. It was a mistake for AMC to take this female couple that was so accepted by mainstream America and separate them as soon as they became happy, and *keep* them apart."

TRIVIA FACTOID: When they were teens, bitchy rich girl Greenlee Smythe nicknamed Erica's daughter "LesBianca." Ok, that's kinda mean, but funny!

QUEER CHARACTER: Twin sisters Mary Frances "Frankie" Stone and Mary Margaret "Maggie" Stone

ACTOR: Elizabeth Hendrickson

THE HOMO HISTORY: Before *All My Children*'s "Lianca" phenomenon began, Erica Kane's lesbian daughter, Bianca Montgomery, experienced her first serious girl-on-girl crush on troubled tomboy Frankie Stone in 2001. Erica disapproved of Bianca's closeness with the pot-smoking, sexually ambiguous Frankie, who broke her daughter's heart by jumping into bed with bad boy JR Chandler. Eventually, Erica stood trial for Frankie's fatal shooting. The devoted diva was just protecting her daughter and she mistakenly assumed that Bianca had slain Frankie for revenge.

Later, Frankie's identical twin, Maggie, showed up in Pine Valley to investigate the murder of her sister. The real killer turned out to be the twins' wicked Aunt Vanessa, who was played by the fabulously campy Marj Dusay. Poor Bianca—who dramatically fainted the first time she saw Maggie—harbored a painful hankering for Frankie's straight look-alike.

For years, the two young women danced around the prospect of becoming more than friends. Maggie once planted a kiss on Bianca and later declared, "I think I'm in love with you." Plus, she often appeared jealous of Bianca's romance with Lena. However, the sexually confused Maggie feared risking the friendship by using Bianca as a guinea pig. Instead, she tended to opt for very dysfunctional relationships with men.

In 2005, actresses Eden Riegel and Elizabeth Hendrickson both decided to leave the New York–based *AMC* to seek other showbiz opportunities in Los Angeles. Thus, Bianca joyfully reclaimed her stolen baby and invited her good pal Maggie to join them in starting a fresh new life in Paris, no strings attached. When the ladies flew off together on a private jet (because soap dykes are too fancy to just rent U-Hauls), it was left unclear whether they were close friends or lovers in the making. However, Bianca later visited Pine Valley sans Maggie and happily informed everyone that they had become an official couple in France. Needless to say, fans of "BAM", short for Bianca and Maggie, were glad, albeit disappointed that Maggie's long-awaited surrender to her bicuriosity had finally happened off-screen.

As the World Turns

QUEER CHARACTER: Hank Elliot
ACTOR: Brian Starcher
THE HOMO HISTORY: Back in 1988, the late, great soap scribe Douglas Marland, created daytime's first gay male character, Hank Elliot. "It was long past the time," Marland said, "to have a leading gay character representing the gay lifestyle on a daytime show."

Colleen Zenk Pinter, who plays Barbara Ryan, recalls Hank's story fondly. "Hank was a young fashion designer that Barbara found in New York," she says. "I brought him back to Oakdale and he worked for me and befriended my teenage son, Paul. One of the women in town had her eye on Hank. He finally revealed both to this female character and to my teenage son that he was gay and that he had a lover, Charles, who was dying of AIDS.

"We almost never saw Charles. He was always off-screen, so you could say that they took the easy way in dealing with the AIDS issue and the gay issue," Zenk Pinter continues, "but not really, because it was the first time that male homosexuality had been dealt with in daytime. They played [Hank] smart. They cast a wonderful actor who was very charismatic, very handsome, and very mainstream. So the audience came to love him and then, oh by the way, guess what? He's gay. So it was kind of a nonissue. [Hank's sexual orientation] was revealed much, much later, which I think, at the time, was the right way to deal with it. And we did not receive any kind of backlash from fans about this because it was handled the right way. The reason Hank left Oakdale was because his lover was dying. I wish we had dealt with the AIDS issue on camera more—we didn't, but at least we talked about it. It was a real groundbreaker back then."

QUEER CHARACTER: Luke Grimaldi Snyder
ACTOR: Van Hansis
THE HOMO HISTORY: Word got out in 2006 that *As the World Turns* intended to have Oakdale teenager Luke come out as a gay boy. This was *big* news for two reasons: For one thing, this show's canvas had been homo-free since Hank Elliot's departure in 1989. Even better, Luke's parents are *ATWT*'s signature supercouple. (Popular soap actors Martha Byrne and Jon Hensley have played his mother, Lily Snyder, and his stepfather, Holden Snyder, since the '80s.) This is very significant because Luke is a young, attractive, established member of a core family in Oakdale, and he came out to parents whom viewers had already known and loved for years.

"*All My Children* did it with Bianca and it worked," says Mimi Torchin, founding editor-in-chief of *Soap Opera Weekly*. "Daytime is a copycat medium, so *AMC* opened the way for other shows to do young, gay characters. We've seen these kids since they were babies and they've been SORASed (that's short for Soap Opera Rapid Aging Syndrome). It integrates a gay teen into the fabric of a show without having to introduce a new character nobody cares about. This way, even if some viewers are slightly uncomfortable, there's an acceptability factor. We feel we *know* these kids. It isn't just an outsider coming in like Michael Delaney or Kevin Sheffield on AMC. Those were islanded characters. A core character like Luke Snyder brings other core characters into the dialogue."

SOAP GOSSIP: Before twenty-two-year-old Van Hansis joined *World Turns*, in 2005, the role of Luke Snyder was played by Jake Weary, the talented fifteen-year-old son of *Guiding Light* grande dame Kim Zimmer (Reva Shayne Lewis). When word got out that Luke would soon be written as a gay character, Zimmer mysteriously pulled her son off the soap. "[Jake's] a sophomore in high school and [*World Turns*] was taking up too much of his real-life time," she later explained on SOAPnet's *Soap Talk*. "He wants to play hockey and do school plays. Our decision had nothing to do with the character being gay. Fans do want to explore that. [Hansis is] a seasoned performer. It'll be better with him."

While not implausible, Zimmer's excuse rang a tad false with some industry wags. "Jake was excellent during the 'Who killed Julia?' story and Luke's kidney transplant story," Torchin points out. "He had plenty of story. It wasn't until the character turned gay that Jake Weary was suddenly working too much."

The Bold and the Beautiful

QUEER CHARACTER: Serge

ACTOR: JM J. Bullock (*Too Close for Comfort, JM J. and Tammy Faye*)

THE HOMO HISTORY: Bullock—the openly gay artist best known as Too Close's sexually ambiguous Monroe Ficus—guest-starred on *B&B* in 2003. He played the super silly and very queeny wedding planner at the umpteenth union of supercouple Brooke and Ridge. "My character's name was Serge," he has said, "but I pronounced it 'Sir-gay.' It's stereotypical, but it was all in fun and jest. I really can't get all hung up on that. Work is work—I'm not in a place where I can be turning things down!"

Days of our Lives

QUEER CHARACTER: Sharon Duval.

ACTOR: Sally Stark

THE HOMO HISTORY: In the steamy '70s, *Days* heroine Julie Olson (Susan Seaforth Hayes) found herself involved in risqué sexual intrigues that had seldom been seen before on daytime soaps. In 1976, the newlywed Julie became friendly with an eccentric neighbor named Sharon Duval, who had recently arrived in Salem along with her rich husband, Karl Duval (Alejandro Rey). As Sharon sat for Julie to have her portrait painted, the colorful Mrs. Duval confided that she was an unhappily married woman. Eventually, Sharon shocked Julie with the news that both she *and* Karl were sexually attracted to her! This sudden introduction of controversial notions like bisexuality and swinging spouses worried NBC's honchos. They reportedly clashed with the late Pat Falken Smith, the head writer of *Days* at the time, which led to the story's swift demise. Julie rejected Sharon, who responded with two suicide attempts. Sharon was then committed to Bayview Sanitarium, where the unenlightened doctors blamed her bicuriosity on her abusive childhood. Meanwhile, the horny Karl used his institutionalized wife's absence to hit on a disinterested Julie, who felt guilty about Sharon's situation. After Sharon was released, she and Karl went off to Europe. But before they departed from Salem forever, Sharon penned an emotional good-bye note, which she left behind for Julie along with the gift of a cameo heirloom. Nobody in Salem dared question the heterosexual status quo again for another quarter of a century.

QUEER CHARACTER: Harold Wentworth
ACTOR: Ryan Scott
THE HOMO HISTORY: *Days* has been jokingly dubbed "The Catholic Hour" for a reason. While the wacky NBC soap is filled with adultery, divorce, and paternity plots, the characters often have religious visions

(Look! It's the Virgin Mary!), and love to judge each other for "sinning against God." So it was quite a pleasant surprise when in 2001 the show introduced Harold, a cute, well-adjusted gay editorial staffer at the local newspaper, *Salem Spectator*. In a totally nonsensical story, Harold developed a crush on screwball journalist Jack Devereaux (Matthew Ashford), who was pretending to be gay, in a misguided effort to win back his ex-wife, Jennifer (Melissa Reeves). After Jack's sitcom-ish ruse ended, Harold served as the gay confidante to a few Salem ladies for a while, then just faded away without explanation.

General Hospital

QUEER CHARACTER: Jon Hanley

ACTOR: Lee Mathis

THE HOMO HISTORY: Back in 1993, Mathis—a gay, HIV-positive actor—desperately placed a situation-wanted ad in the Hollywood trade-paper *Variety*, stating that he needed work to keep his union health benefits. "Friends said it would ruin my career," Mathis told *Entertainment Weekly*. "But I figured, f— it, I need the benefits." Surprisingly, the ad scored Mathis a couple of small film parts and a recurring role on *General Hospital* as Jon Hanley, a longtime pal of the divalicious Lucy Coe (Lynn Herring). Like his portrayer, Jon was a gay man with HIV. (He was also the first openly gay character in the soap's history.) Jon's biggest function was to help Lucy organize the annual Nurses' Ball, which

GH staged each June 21, the Day of Compassion, to raise AIDS awareness. At the 1996 Nurses' Ball, Lucy sadly announced that Jon Hanley had died of AIDS, just as Lee Mathis had done in real life on May 1, of that year. Mathis was only forty-four years old.

QUEER CHARACTER: Ted Murty
ACTOR: Patrick Fabian
THE HOMO HISTORY: On Valentine's Day 1997, *GH* good girl Elizabeth Webber (Rebecca Herbst) was walking home after her school's V-Day dance, only to be brutally raped by a stranger in the park. Liz, and her boyfriend Lucky (Jonathan Jackson), then went on a quest to suss out the identity of her unknown attacker. In a weird twist, Liz suspected her English teacher, Ted Murty, and went to his home to accuse him. Once there, she discovered that Mr. Murty was gay and had a male lover. The fact of his homosexuality was apparently sufficient proof of Mr. Murty's innocence. Liz moved on with her investigation, and *GH*'s gay teacher was forgotten about.

QUEER CHARACTER: Elton Herbert
ACTOR: Loren Freeman
THE HOMO HISTORY: The sissified wedding planner is a stereotypical stock character on soap operas, which owes its origins to the prissy, officious "sissy" roles played by Edward Everett Horton and Franklin Pangborn in '30s comedy films. For better or worse, Loren Freeman is an actor in that old-fashioned

dandy tradition.

Back in 2001, Ned Ashton and Alexis Davis (Wally Kurth, Nancy Lee Grahn) hired Elton, as played by Freeman, to orchestrate a fancy, frilly matrimonial event with all the trimmings. Elton's stay in Port Charles was extended with a job as the sassy secretarial sidekick to Laura Spencer (Genie Francis) at Deception Cosmetics. Elton's scenes typically included campy lines like this: "Come now! Remember, modeling is more than hair extensions and sunglasses!"

QUEER CHARACTER: Lucas Jones

ACTOR: Ben Hogestyn

THE HOMO HISTORY: Lucas is the adopted son of two beloved *GH* characters, Dr. Tony Jones (Brad Maule), and Nurse Bobbie Spencer (Jackie Zeman), an ex-prostitute who became a medicine woman after retiring from the world's oldest profession. In 2005, Lucas slowly and cautiously began coming out to family and friends. He later outed himself to the whole town of Port Charles after his violent altercation with Frank, a local gay basher. Bobbie couldn't believe her son's revelation at first— "Spencer men are supposed to be macho!"—and suggested he might need psychological counseling. Ultimately, though, the loving mom stuck by Lucas with her signature spunk.

In one beautifully played scene, Tony was very accepting and loving, when Lucas came out to him. Too bad Tony died from a mysterious tropical virus in their next father-son scene! Lucas sure could've used his dad's continued support. Fortunately, he has found a friend and a role model in the out and proud Guy, who also survived a run-in with Frank, the gay basher. Significantly, Guy urged Lucas to press charges against his attacker and emphasized that silence equals death, when it comes to facing homophobia.

LUKE SPENCER SPEAKS OUT: Gay teen Lucas has another strong supporter in his famous uncle, Luke Spencer, who has saved Port Charles—and the world—from evildoers more than once. "Luke told him, 'You're perfect the way you are. Spencers make their own rules in the world. Don't ever bow to ignorance, don't ever apologize to anybody for who you are or who you love,'" recalls *GH* superstar Anthony Geary, who plays Luke. "I've really appreciated that point of view, because I think it's important to have a character with Luke's gravitas say these things. Luke is also his uncle, so it's important. I think Luke appreciates Lucas in a new light. He is his own man. Luke always liked rule breakers who make their own way. That's what Luke's all about. I think he sees his nephew in that category and very much respects him for being who he is."

Geary is enthused that *GH* is finally including a central gay character in its continuing saga. "It's high time," he says. "It's part of the world we live in. I am very, very tired of having people with limited information, and a lot of hatred, tell the rest of us how we're supposed to feel. I'm sick to death of it. So if we can, through a story or a character, make the smallest contribution to balancing the world's view of these issues, I'm all for it."

SOAP GOSSIP: You read on page 110 that *As the World Turns* had to recast a character when an actor left the soap, just as a gay story line was about to commence. The same thing happened on *GH* in the same year. Actor Ryan Carnes quit playing Lucas soon after news broke that *GH* would be exploring Lucas's sexual orientation. Although Carnes's rep denied it, the word was that he feared being typecast as a guy who only plays gays. He was already making regular appearances on *Desperate Housewives*, as Justin, the gay gardener who was dating Bree Van De Kamp's son, Andrew. Carnes had also played the love interest of openly gay *American Idol* finalist Jim Verraros in Q. Allan Brocka's indie comedy *Eating Out*. Carnes's carnal activities in the movie included full-frontal nudity and the enthusiastic performance of oral sex on another man. Oh, and get this: His character's porn star-ish name was Marc Everhard. Yes, really.

Whatever the reason for Carnes's exit, the role was recast with cute daytime newcomer Ben Hogestyn, who happens to be the stepson of popular *Days of our Lives* star Drake Hogestyn (John Black).

Mary Hartman, Mary Hartman
QUEER CHARACTERS: Ed and Howard McCullough
ACTORS: Larry Haddon, Beeson Carroll
THE HOMO HISTORY: Legendary TV producer Norman

Lear (*All in the Family, The Jeffersons, Maude*) debuted the popular, syndicated soap satire *Mary Hartman, Mary Hartman* in 1976. *The Wall Street Journal* called it "the funniest show in the history of television" at the time. The show's titular buck-toothed housewife heroine (Louise Lasser) encountered many colorful characters in her hometown of Fernwood, Ohio. The queerest? Her neighbors, Ed and Howard McCullough, turned out to be gay lovers, who were posing as brothers for the sake of suburban propriety. Soap vet Gloria DeHaven (*Ryan's Hope, Falcon Crest*) also appeared occasionally as a lesbian neighbor called Annie "Tippytoes" Wylie. On a supergay side note, '50s matinee idol Tab Hunter—who recently came out in his memoir *Tab Hunter Confidential*—joined the *Hartman* spin-off *Forever Fernwood*, as Mary's recast father, George Schumway. In typical soapy style, it was explained that George (originally played by Philip Bruns) had undergone drastic plastic surgery from head to toe after falling into a vat of Rust-Oleum.

One Life to Live

QUEER CHARACTER: Billy Douglas
ACTOR: Ryan Phillippe
THE HOMO HISTORY: Long before Ryan Phillippe became the Hollywood matinee idol also known as Mr. Reese Witherspoon, he got his big break on *One Life*, at age seventeen. Viewers were introduced to the actor in 1992 as Billy Douglas, a closeted

gay teen whose life seemed outwardly perfect: He was well-to-do, blond, and gorgeous—those sensuous, romantic lips!—and served as captain of his high-school swim team and class president. Because Billy felt confused and isolated like many queer kids, he brought his coming out issues to the understanding Reverend Andrew Carpenter (Wortham Krimmer), at St. James Church.

Enter the emotionally messy Marty Saybrooke (Susan Haskell), who resented the pastor's repeated rejections of her slutty advances. One day, Marty spied Andrew putting a fatherly hand on Billy's shoulder to comfort him. Jealous Marty then spitefully ran to Billy's WASPy parents, William and Virginia, and twisted the innocent gesture. In the version Marty told them, Andrew had tried to seduce their son. Uh oh! That lie lead Billy's homophobic father to incite the townsfolk of Llanview into a very ugly hate campaign.

Since Andrew's late brother, also named William, was a gay man who had died of AIDS, the pastor refused to appease local bigots by publicly affirming his heterosexuality. Like a truly brave Christian, Andrew proudly withstood the same kinds of discrimination gays face, including a brutal bashing, as well as pressure to quit his job at St. James.

In an historic move, *One Life*'s then-executive producer Linda Gottlieb arranged for the then 20,000-panel Names Project AIDS Memorial Quilt to be featured on the show. In the story, Andrew invited the quilt to come to St. James Church in

Llanview, so that he could preach a special sermon about human compassion and add a panel in memory of his brother. (The quilt sequences were actually filmed on location at the Church of Christ the King in New Vernon, New Jersey.) Andrew's proposed event initially angered his own bigoted father, Sloan Carpenter (Roy Thinnes), who planned to boycott the ceremony like Billy's dad.

Fortunately, Sloan attended anyway. Not only did he make peace with Andrew, he finally acknowledged the truth about his gay son, William, and mourned his loss.

As for Billy, the teen publicly came out right after Andrew's sermon. Billy's mom, Virginia, was so moved by her son's words that she bear hugged him. "Nothing could ever make me stop loving you!" Virginia declared. "Nothing in this world!"

QUEER CHARACTER: Mark Solomon
ACTOR: Matt Cavenaugh
THE HOMO HISTORY: Flashback to the summer of 2004. In a scenario just like MTV's *The Real World*, eight Llanview University students from different backgrounds moved in together for a community-service project. Although their coed cottage was called the Love Center, some of the housemates weren't too loving when the shy, stand off-ish Mark Solomon worked up the nerve to out himself to them. Arrogant jock Nick (Will Bozarth), said he wasn't comfortable rooming with a gay guy. Mark's response? "Relax, I'm into brains anyway. I'd never be attracted to you." Yup,

STRAIGHT ALLY: *ONE LIFE TO LIVE'S* KATHY BRIER (MARCIE)

SOAP OPERAS are about family and friendship as much as they are about fantasy and romance. So it has been heartwarming to see an earthy, relatable young woman like Marcie Walsh McBain stick up for her gay pal, Mark, and work so hard to make her gay brother, Eric, and his husband, James, feel included in the Walsh clan. Marcie's messages of loving acceptance have no doubt touched many real lives on the other side of the TV screen. Who better to deliver Marcie's words

of wisdom than Kathy Brier, who has played Tracy Turnblad in *Hairspray* on Broadway?

"The concept of homophobia is so odd and foreign to me," admits Brier. "It's hard to wrap my head around it because I don't get it. I definitely think it is important to talk about it on soap operas, though."

How did Marcie, a woman raised by an old-fashioned Irish Catholic father, come to be so open-minded? "Marcie was an outsider in her own family," Brier responds. "She was the only girl in a family of guys and she also happened to look like her dead mother, so her father could never really get too close to Marcie. It was painful for him. She wasn't one of the boys and she felt left out. So Marcie and Eric felt a connection and became good friends. They bonded over not knowing exactly where they fit in. They were kindred spirits and soulmates, in a way. Marcie totally adores Eric. By the way, Bill Dawes, who plays Eric, is one of the best young actors I've played opposite. Props to him!

"When their father, Charlie Walsh, rejected Eric because he didn't understand homosexuality and gay marriage, Marcie knew what it felt like for Eric to not feel a part of their family. That's why Marcie supports Eric for who he is. Although even if those unfortunate circumstances *didn't* exist in the family, I think Marcie would support Eric anyway. She's not a homophobic person.

"In one episode, we had really good scenes where Marcie and her fiancé, Michael McBain (Nathaniel Marston), were discussing gay marriage," Brier recalls. "Those scenes were originally written between Marcie and her gay friend, Mark Solomon. I went upstairs to the producers and said, "I think this conversation is important to have on a soap opera. But for Marcie to have this conversation with a gay man, it falls flat because it's preaching to the choir. It doesn't give you heated discussion with a character who is uncomfortable with gay marriage.

"I didn't do it because I wanted to take the material away from Matt Cavenaugh, who played Mark," she adds. "I just thought that the conversation would take on a more important meaning if Michael, a straight guy character, did the scene with Marcie. Plus, it added a new emotional level because our families are so important to us. Marcie basically said, 'How do I love a man who is not comfortable with accepting my gay brother, who is my best friend?' That sure brought Michael around!"

Mark found his personality in a hurry once the ice was broken. Sweet-natured, spunky redhead Marcie Walsh (Kathy Brier) helped Mark school their classmates in tolerance and everything was eventually copasetic with the kids.

QUEER CHARACTER: Eric Walsh
ACTOR: Bill Dawes
THE HOMO HISTORY: Not long after her friend Mark Solomon came out at the Love Center, Marcie Walsh (Kathy Brier) also lent support to her gay brother, Eric, who was engaged to marry his partner, James. Talk about a cute couple! Sadly, the matrimonial news met with severe disapproval from Marcie's father, Charlie, and her other brother, Ron. Charlie even threatened to disown Marcie if she continued to be supportive of Eric! With some nudging from Marcie, however, the Walsh family gathered together and made peace over dinner on Father's Day in June 2005. Eric's dad praised him for being "a good, decent man" and swore he was done judging his son for whom he loved. It was significant that, when the Walshes sat down to dine together, Charlie sat at the head of the table with son Eric at his right hand and James, Eric's husband-to-be, on the other.

QUEER CHARACTER: Daniel Colson
ACTOR: Mark Dobies
THE HOMO HISTORY: In 2003, Llanview lady lawyer Nora Hanen (Hillary Bailey Smith) lost the election for Llantano County district attorney to a politically

ambitious loudmouth, Daniel Colson. Nora seemed as surprised as *One Life*'s viewers were, when she accepted her abrasive campaign rival's marriage proposal and wed him. Soon, there was a big murder mystery after someone shot Paul Cramer, an opportunistic, baby-switching scumbag, who was played by *One Life* star Heather Tom's hottie brother, David Tom.

It was later revealed that Daniel Colson was a closet gay man and had gunned down Paul for blackmailing him with that explosive personal info. Daniel had also used a trash bag to suffocate his son Riley's girlfriend, the blonde beauty Jennifer Rappaport (Jessica Morris), effectively snuffing out the truth about his sexual orientation and his culpability in Paul's murder. This wasn't the first time poor Nora had romanced a murderer, but she was still sickened by Daniel's endless lies and cover-ups. The rest of Llanview was also shocked by the D.A.'s cold-blooded crimes, especially Daniel's secret boyfriend, Llanview U. student Mark Solomon. "So he was the unknown party on the other end of Daniel's mysterious telephone calls!" we realized. Although Mark knew he was dating a closeted, married man and urged him to come clean with Nora, Daniel's naïve boy toy obviously had no clue how far his lover had gone to hide their affair.

Needless to say, major controversy ensued! "It's a rehash of the familiar closeted gay, self-loathing killer story," griped a spokesman for GLAAD (Gay & Lesbian Alliance Against Defamation), which had previously lauded *One Life* for Mark's coming out story. "There are certainly more creative, less stereotypical stories that could have been told about a gay, married politician with a grown son."

While this tale wasn't the most politically correct, it undeniably made for can't-miss compelling drama. *One Life* head writer Dena Higley said the Daniel Colson story was a takeoff on the real-life scandal of disgraced New Jersey Governor Jim McGreevey, who resigned his lofty office after confessing to an affair with a male employee and publicly apologizing to his wife and the state. Of course, McGreevey didn't physically harm anyone to hide his sexual secret, but Higley has said she had to "amp up the stakes" for the sake of juicy soap opera. Additionally, *One Life* sent a message through various characters' dialogue that Daniel's crimes of deception and murder were objectionable, but his sexual orientation was not.

Passions

QUEER CHARACTER: Simone Russell

ACTOR: Cathy Jeneén Doe

THE HOMO HISTORY: The youngest daughter of Harmony's main African-American family, the Russells, Simone lived in the shadow of her beautiful, popular big sister, Whitney. She whined and bitched about Whit as frequently as Jan Brady used to cry "Marcia, Marcia, Marcia!" on *The Brady Bunch*. Later, Simone grew up, matured into a pretty young woman and finally got the town's notice by bravely coming out as a lesbian. Without much publicity, protest, or fanfare at all, *Passions* has shown Simone sharing a few very steamy kisses with her on-and-off girlfriend, Rae, as played by Latina beauty Josarra Jinaro. Whether the soap will give Simone a fully realized, ongoing relationship with a woman remains to be seen.

Santa Barbara

QUEER CHARACTERS: Channing Capwell, Jr., and Lindsay Smith

ACTORS: Robert Brian Wilson and Joel Bailey

THE HOMO HISTORY: *Santa Barbara* debuted on July 30, 1984, with a whodunit surrounding the fatal shooting of Californian playboy Channing Capwell, Jr., five years prior. As the mystery unfolded, it was revealed that many lovers, including his father's mistress, and a person called Lindsay Smith, had pleasured Channing. Turns out, Lindsay was a man! Channing's homoluscious relationship with Lindsay was established in a 1985 flashback. This was a scandalous scooplet of soap gossip back in the day!

A Q CLOSE-UP WITH

Eden Riegel

EDEN RIEGEL has scored herself a deeply devoted fan following—plus a Daytime Emmy trophy for outstanding younger actress—as Erica Kane's out and proud lesbian daughter, Bianca Montgomery, on *All My Children*. Who would've imagined that anyone would become a major afternoon suds star by playing a gay role? Talk about progress. Here, Riegel dishes the continuing phenom that is Bianca!

Soaps were originally meant to entertain heterosexual housewives. Yet your character's same-sex romances have been wildly popular with both straight and gay viewers.

I was surprised. I think everybody was surprised. Everybody thought *All My Children* was taking a big gamble by making Erica Kane's daughter a lesbian. They didn't know how it would be received by the fans, but the fans have been amazing. It is definitely because the show told Bianca's story so sensitively. They really got the audience to love my character through Erica Kane. That was the key. They feel this is Susan Lucci's daughter and everybody watched her grow up. Since everybody identifies with Erica, they sort of see Bianca as *their* daughter. So because of that, they were much more accepting of the fact that she was a lesbian and went along with the story, which I was thrilled about. I don't know that anybody expected it. I certainly didn't. When I started and signed a however-many-year contract, I was like, "Yeah right. Nobody ever survives on soaps that long!" But the audience embraced my character, so I've found a home at *All My Children*, which I'm really very grateful for.

Family really is key on soaps. As long as you make a character the kin of someone we care about, we're willing to accept them as anything, even a space alien. Not to compare lesbians with space aliens ... well, you know what I mean.

[Laughs] Yes, I do know what you mean. It's funny you say that, because the day Bianca came out, I was wearing a space alien costume! It was the Halloween episode.

Hilarious! It seems AMC's strategy to gain sympathy for Bianca was to have her victimized a lot. Of course, all soap heroines must suffer, but Bianca really suffered!

Yeah, she certainly did! I was thrilled. I thought I'd hit the trifecta when I got raped, had a baby, and then killed my rapist. I see that as the greatest story ever! [*Laughs*] That's because I was looking at it from an actor's point of view and not necessarily an advocate's point of view.

If Bianca were always cheery and peaceful, it wouldn't make for very compelling drama.

Nobody's happy on soaps. It's really boring. If they are happy, they're happy for a day and then the audience is like, "OK, we're ready for something else to happen!"

Although you're seeking your fortunes outside daytime TV, the soap fans feel it's gracious that you still return to Pine Valley for occasional visits.

Oh, that's really sweet to say, but I feel like I'm the lucky one. I've got a great deal going! Bianca is a role that I really love. I love being there at *All My Children*. The cast members are like my family. It's amazing that the show is allowing me to pursue my dreams, see what else is out there and enjoy my youth, but still keep the door open to come back and make visits now and again. I really appreciate it—and I'll do it as long as they let me!

ACCLAIMED ACTOR, SCREENWRITER, AND FILM
DIRECTOR CHARLES BUSCH HAD A SHORT-TERM GIG
ON ABC'S *ONE LIFE TO LIVE*, AS "PEG BARLOW."
(COURTESY OF DAVID RODGERS)

Gender Bending on *One Life to Live*

QUOTE

> "If I don't straighten up, someone else will be playing my part tomorrow!"

CHARLES BUSCH is a fantabulously talented actor, playwright, novelist, screenwriter, director, and legendary drag performer. He authored Broadway's hit play *The Tale of the Allergist's Wife* and the semi-autobiographical novel *Whores of Lost Atlantis*. Busch also wrote and starred in the comedic films *Psycho Beach Party* and *Die Mommie Die*. Here, in his own witty words, he recalls his nine-episode stint as Peg Barlow, a female character on *One Life to Live*.

"I think it was October of 2001. My manager called up with a great air of surprise and said, '*One Life to Live* contacted us and said they want you to play this lady who runs a modeling agency.' I was immediately dubious. I said, 'Yeah? Well, find out first which episode they'll want to pull my wig off so they can reveal, 'She's a man!'" I've never played a *Some Like It Hot*-type of role and I've never done anything with a plot in which I was a man posing as a woman. I play *female* characters. If the idea is to pull my wig off and then I'm revealed to be a man, I won't do it.

"So my manager called me back and said, 'They just think it'd be fun casting for you to play this Kay Thompson in a *Funny Face*-type of flamboyant lady who runs a modeling agency.' They wanted me to play a real lady, and suddenly, I had all these visions of the Dustin Hoffman film *Tootsie* in my head!

"I called up the show's then-executive producer, Gary Tomlin, and he said, 'You can tweak your own dialogue if you want.' I said, 'The first thing I'd like to tweak is my character's name, Sasha." That name implied a foreigner to me, and I'm a real American kinda gal. The kinda lady I do is one part Roz Russell, one part Susan Hayward, and I don't know who else.

"I could hear Gary Tomlin sigh like, 'Oh God, what have I got myself into?' on the other end. He said, 'What would you like the character to be called?' So I said, 'Peg Barlow!' It had a sharp, efficient, strong career woman kind of vibe to it. Then when they sent the script over, I said, 'You know, in my first episode, nobody ever says her name. When I first enter, and introduce myself to Jen, that's Jessica Morris, the young girl whose character enters my hot modeling agency—'could I introduce myself and say, 'Margaret Barlow. Call me Peg.'" So he says, 'Okaaaaaay.' I could just imagine him rolling his eyes on the other line.

"So then I went in to see the *One Life to Live* costume people at the studio. They were so sweet and we were all on the same page, trying to find chic, smart business suits. What I wasn't prepared for though, is how the world of soaps goes so slowly. I think that the nine episodes I was there took place over the course of two days in Llanview time. You're wearing the same clothes the whole time. They finally decided to pretend that I was going to go out for cocktails later in the evening to get me into a second outfit! I wondered, "Is there ever a morning?" One of the actresses there told me she was in bed with a man for two weeks! It was such a strange, exotic world to be thrown into.

The interesting thing is that I had scenes with this really cute boy, and I can't remember his name because I came back on a Monday after being off for the weekend and they said, "So-and-so who was playing Al isn't going to be on today. He was fired over the weekend and he's being replaced." Suddenly, I'm in the scene, and a strange person walked through the door and an announcer said, "The character of Al is now being played by Nathaniel Marston."

It was terrifying. I thought, "Oh my God, they move so quickly here. If I don't straighten up, someone else will be playing my part tomorrow!"

I thought I was just so dreadful at soap acting, because I was so green at the whole thing. But on my last day there the assistant director said, in a thick New York accent, "Oh, we're gonna miss you. You really saved our asses." I said, "You're kidding." I guess being from the theater, I took for granted things like a director saying, "Oh, just do something," in a scene. That means improvise. At one point, Peg Barlow had to be chattering in the background giving orders to

Q

Soap Gender Benders

1. Who played the first male-to-female transgender character on a daytime soap?

   a. Charles Busch
   b. RuPual
   c. Carlotta Chang
   d Anne Heche

2. Which *One Life to Live* character hired a drag queen as a bartender?

   a. Dorian Lord
   b. RJ Gannon
   c. Victoria Lord Davidson
   d. Mitch Laurence

3. Which reality TV star played Sami Brady's male alter ego "Stan" on *Days of our Lives* in 2005?

   a. The Real World: Chicago's *Kyle Brandt*
   b. The Bachelorette's *Ryan Sutter*
   c. American Idol's *Ryan Seacrest*
   d. Boy Meets Boy's *Dan Wells*

Soap Gender Benders

4. What was the drag name Cass Winthrop (Stephen Schnetzer) used when cross-dressing on *Another World*?

   a. *Tamara Knight*
   b. *Krystal Lake*
   c. *Iona Farmhouse*
   d. *Devoida Sense*

5. Which female character in the 1991 spoof *Soapdish* was born a man?

   a. *Celeste Talbert*
   b. *Montana Moorehead*
   c. *Rose Schwartz*
   d. *Lori Craven*

all her minions and I just improvised a whole long monologue and then had to repeat it several times. That was considered acting of the highest caliber!

"The other thing I thought was peculiar was the first day I was there. I walked into the makeup room and saw all these well-known stage actresses from the '70s, who had disappeared. I'd never heard of them for twenty-five years and I didn't realize soaps were like the Witness Protection Program. There was Patricia

Elliott, who plays Renee Buchanan on *One Life to Live*, Pamela Peyton Wright, who plays Addie Cramer, and some others. I thought, 'So *this* is where they've been hiding out all these years. And they're gettin' a lot of money!'

"The most disappointing thing was going online to a *One Life to Live* chat room to see what people were saying about me. A number of people wrote in wondering, 'When will Jen figure out that Peg's a man?' I was so disappointed, but it sort of made sense because when drag is used, it's usually part of the plot. Someone's *posing* as a woman or a man. What we were doing was such a radical thing, in a sense, having a man playing this female part with no explanation. To the ordinary person, it could be confusing.

"When we watched the first episode, my lover, Eric, was surprised that they don't do any retakes unless you make a *really* big blunder. In my first entrance on the show, I tripped over the telephone cord and they kept the camera going!

I was so nervous about forgetting lines. I thought there'd be a TelePrompTer and there *isn't* one. Eric asked me, 'How come you're takin' a breath after every third word?'' I was like, ''Cause I don't know what the *fourth* word is!'

"My dialogue would be like, 'Jen, why don't you . . . come over here and . . . give me your resume.' I was *very* nervous.

"I felt just like Faye Dunaway as Joan Crawford in the movie *Mommie Dearest*, when Joan goes on the old soap opera *The Secret Storm* to play her daughter Christina's role. Everything I do has a double edge, like in my film *Die Mommie Die*. It didn't escape me that I was like this great actress reduced to doing a soap opera. I was very relieved when the nine episodes were over because I didn't even have much to do, but I found it just too nerve-wracking to have to memorize things quickly. I have such admiration for these people who have huge scenes to do each day, the way they absorb so much material. I don't know how they do it. They do have wonderful actors on these soaps."

OUT AND PROUD ARTIST THOM BIERDZ PLAYED
"PHILLIP CHANCELLOR III" ON CBS'S *THE YOUNG AND
THE RESTLESS* IN THE LATE 1980S. (COURTESY OF
MARINA RICE BADER)

CHAPTER NINE

The Daytime Closet

QUOTE

"You can't go into an audition gay—and by that, I mean you can't go in effeminate."

GOSSIP, GOSSIP, GOSSIP! It's a big business in our celebrity-obsessed country. Fortunes and careers are made by dishing the stars' sordid scandals and secrets to the hungrily voyeuristic public. Their break-ups, affairs, addictions, personal feuds, and such are all considered fair game. Tabloids even devote full pages to paparazzi shots of celebs caught eating! (How would you like millions of Americans to giggle over a candid shot of you stuffing an ooey-gooey, messy burrito into your mouth? Not glamorous.) It seems no star is totally safe from facing indecent exposure and embarrassment in the public eye at some point in his or her career.

Well, no A-list star is safe, anyway.

Those B-, C-, and D-listers have serious cause for concern, too. But our soap stars—whether fortunately or unfortunately—come in dead last in the celebrity pecking order. With very few exceptions, like *All My Children*'s Susan Lucci, actors who make their living on soap operas are off the tabloids' radar. Only occasionally will you see TV shows like *Entertainment Tonight, Extra,* or *Access Hollywood* devote airtime to a story involving soap stars. And they usually have to be doing something extraordinary—like suing the late Aaron Spelling or donating bone marrow to a dying child—to warrant tabloid TV attention in the form of a thirty-second sound bite. On rare occasions, *ET* and the rest might do a behind-the-scenes story from a soap's set, for use as filler on a slow news day.

The reason soaps and their stars are largely ignored by the mainstream media is because soap ratings are in decline. The Nielsen ratings are nowhere near the level they were in the early '80s, when *General Hospital*'s Genie Francis appeared on the covers of major publications like *Newsweek*. From a business standpoint, there's simply not enough demand out there for the media to supply hardcore gossip and speculation about soap stars' personal lives.

Which is exactly why it's so easy for gay soap actors to remain in the closet. The only mass media outlets that regularly cover daytime soaps and their stars are *TV Guide* magazine and TVGuide.com, and the three weekly soap magazines, *Soaps In Depth, Soap Opera Digest,* and *Soap Opera Weekly*. The relationship between the soap press and the nine daytime dramas currently on the air, is very much like that of the movie magazines and movie studios of the '40s. During the days of Hollywood's studio system, the press kissed the studios' tushes—or the press got no access to the stars. Yes, there was gossip, but the press kept much more scandalous information secret than they ever reported. It's very much the same way with today's soap-opera press.

"The mainstream press still doesn't care about soap actors very much," says Mimi Torchin, founding editor-in-chief of *Soap Opera Weekly*. "The soap press is going to protect them. It's just what we do. We don't out our stars. We respect the privacy of the people we cover. If they don't want to say that they're gay or lesbian, it's not our job to reveal that. Most of the soap fans don't want to know that stuff anyway."

A highly famous veteran soap star agrees. This gentleman—who has played many leading-man roles on daytime and nighttime soaps—agreed to be interviewed for this book only on the condition of anonymity. "If any actor is out publicly, that actor will not be accepted by the audience as somebody who likes to passionately make love to women," he states. "It's a sad fact, but it's a true one. When you're somebody in front of a camera about whom the audience has sexual fantasies and you're gay, you've got to be quiet about it and for very good reason. The public confuses actors with their characters. If you decide to come out, make sure you've got your money together and you can afford to."

"There are still an awful lot of Hollywood actors that aren't out," Torchin adds. "I agree with people who feel that every time somebody comes out, it helps the cause. However, I don't think that gay people have the responsibility to out themselves in a climate that isn't receptive. As long as it might still hurt their careers, they don't have the responsibility to do something just for the greater good of mankind."

"The irony is that there are *a lot* of gay people in daytime," says Michael Bruno, an openly gay talent manager who reps many soap stars and also appears as a judge on SOAPnet's *I Wanna Be a Soap Star*. "It's very gay friendly and gay actors are hired. I would say there are currently maybe thirty lesbian and gay male actors working on soaps. Everybody in the industry knows about them.

"The interesting thing about it is—and some people will call me a self-hating fag for this—I find myself being very, very careful with the boys who come into my office wanting representation. I'll say to some of them, 'It's unfortunate, really, because it does hurt me to do this, but I just don't think you're gonna get work.' You can't go into an audition gay—and by that, I mean you can't go in effeminate.

"You can't go into an audition for *All My Children* or *One Life to Live* where they know immediately that you are gay. You can't do it. You will not get to the next step. You will not screen test; therefore, you will not get the job. Daytime is essentially for women in the Midwest. The fans want their leading men to like leading women. They don't want to know that this guy might like guys. For the younger actors, specifically, I think it is a detriment to come out. And I get a lot of crap for saying that, but I'm in the business.

"So do you come out before you get an acting job— therefore you don't get a job—so it does nothing and you have no platform to speak from? Until you're in daytime, you really can't make a statement because no one's going to listen. Or do you wait until you're on TV and, at some point, say, 'This is who I am and let the chips fall where they may.' "

Will daytime TV ever see a hot soap hunk, or babe, come out while he or she is still working on a soap? "When that happens, it's going to be an enormous breakthrough," Bruno muses. "I am very curious to see who the first twenty- to thirty-something young leading man will be that says, 'I'm gay.' I think that's when the tide will turn. Because I don't think they'll get fired at that point. If they're fired [for being gay], all hell will break loose. And we'll see."

A *Young and the Restless* alumnus, Thom Bierdz, is the only well-known soap-opera stud who has come out "officially"—meaning he consented to be profiled in the respected queer newsmagazine *The Advocate*, a basic rite of passage for most openly gay celebs in America. Of course, that was in 2003, years after he'd left daytime TV. Bierdz had really sizzled on *Y&R*'s front burner from 1986-89 in the role of troubled teen alcoholic Phillip Chancellor III. Phillip was coupled up with the top-rated soap's sweetheart, Christine "Cricket" Blair, who continues to be played by Lauralee Bell, the daughter of *Y&R* creators Lee Phillip and William J. Bell. Bierdz, who is still boyishly handsome at forty-one, has since become a gay role model as an out and proud award-winning visual artist, whose paintings sell quite well. FYI, he was the one and *only* gay daytime actor who agreed to be quoted on the record for this book.

"I can understand people being inspired by me," Bierdz says, without a hint of ego. "I don't think it was

SO YOU WANNA BE A GAY SOAP STAR

SSSH! Unfortunately, the daytime closet door is still slammed shut. When it comes to auditioning for soap roles, *I Wanna Be a Soap Star* judge and talent manager Michael Bruno warns that women should appear femme and men must seem masculine. If you're a gay boy with leading man aspirations, Bruno has a few tips to help keep you from tipping off casting directors that you're a big ol' homo. If an actor reads as gay during an audition for a soap-hunk role, he says, "you're gonna get screwed. They're gonna say, 'I don't know if the Midwest is gonna believe him playing opposite a woman.'" Warning: Bruno's candid advice isn't the most politically correct, but his star-studded client roster is proof that he knows how actors do and don't land roles in Hollywood.

1. An FYI to fierce fashionistas who dress for success: The "metrosexual" look is *so* over. "One thing I'll say to guys is, 'Mess yourself up a little bit.' Straight guys, for the most part, *don't know* what T-shirt looks best with those jeans and these boots and exactly how much beard shadow looks good on your face. I say, 'Just put stuff in your hair and go.'"

2. Well groomed is OK, but *too* groomed says gay, gay, gay! "I can always tell gay boys—the eyebrows are always perfectly tweezed. It's a dead giveaway. If you look too 'done,' like you've spent too much time at it, people start to question."

3. Just because it worked for James Dean—*allegedly*—don't try to use sex as a shortcut to stardom. "Daytime soaps want beefcake. They want hot models turned actors," Bruno says. "People who represent these actors may hit on you and they're gonna promise things, thinking they'll get something in return. You *never* compromise yourself. Flirting never hurts, but if you go too far, it's gonna bite you in the ass."

my talent or looks that got me on *The Young and the Restless*, although I did resemble Tom Cruise, who was hot at that time, and soaps always copy what's hot in pop culture. I think it was my drive—I had a fierce drive. Gay people can have that drive and they can achieve. I hope that that's inspiring, and that they don't limit themselves because other people limit them."

Bierdz, who always knew he was gay, couldn't always afford to be so open and honest about his life. "I'm from Kenosha, Wisconsin," he says. "When I was nineteen, I started bartending at gay bars in Milwaukee, Wisconsin. So there I was working in my cowboy hat—and whatever mustache I could grow—in a gay bar! I came out to Los Angeles at twenty-one, and I was bussing tables at a gay restaurant in the Silver Lake neighborhood. That's where I was introduced to my future manager. Jim said it wouldn't be advisable to be out, although I wanted to be out. The producers at *The Young and the Restless*, or any soap, wouldn't have hired an openly gay actor in 1986. There was homophobia and a big fear of AIDS at that time. It was talked about as a gay disease. They were afraid that people in the Bible Belt wouldn't watch a gay actor and that advertisers would pull away their money. It was understood that they would rather just cast 'straight' guys.

"I thought nobody knew I was gay at *Y&R* and I was trying to keep that a secret," Bierdz continues. "I couldn't be out, but I didn't want to lie. I did bring a girl date to one or two *Y&R* events. I also remember going to personal appearances at malls and places like that. One time, there were 7,000 girls screaming for me at a Toronto mall. They asked if I had a girlfriend. I said no and they screamed very happily. I didn't tell them my boyfriend was there!"

Just like gay and lesbian soap actors still do today, Bierdz kept the romantic details of his personal life opaque when talking to the soap-opera press. "I remember being interviewed by *Soap Opera Digest* for my first magazine cover," he says with a chuckle. "They asked what kind of girl I was interested in, and I tried to avoid pronouns. I said, 'I like somebody who has this or somebody who likes to do that.' The female reporter caught on and she started to avoid the pronouns, too. I remember wrestling with what to say because I didn't want to hurt my career. Looking back, it would not have hurt me one bit to come out, in the sense that I left *Y&R* after my three-year contract was up, anyway. But it was a difficult time to be out and gay."

Bierdz admits he did enjoy a very sweet setside romance during his Y&R days. "About a year into my run on the show, I was looking for a boyfriend," he recalls with a smile. "I became infatuated with the show's florist, who was named Dante. We had eye contact. He put an orchid in my dressing room and asked me out. Then I had him over for dinner and we dated for a while, like ten months. No, we never had sex in my dressing room. Today I would! But back then, nothing happened. That's one story you may not know, as far as gay soap trivia goes!"

Will any of daytime's queer leading men ever come out as a hunky homo? Will a lipstick lesbian leading lady open up about her lady-loving ways?

And if so, will modern viewers simply get over it and let those openly gay actors keep on playing straight soap romances, just like they always have? As suds fans know, long-buried secrets always have a way of coming out. Tune in tomorrow . . .

ANSWERS TO QUIZZES

Q Quiz #1: Soap History

1. b. Nikki Reed, *The Young and the Restless*. Nikki caught gonorrhea from a teenage tryst with Paul Williams back in the '70s.
2. c. 1991.
3. a. *Search for Tomorrow* was thirty-five years old when NBC canceled it in 1986.
4. d. Soap godmother Irna Phillips created the radio soap *Painted Dreams* in 1930. She is the creator of sudsers like *As the World Turns, Another World, Guiding Light, Days of our Lives, The Brighter Day,* and *Love Is a Many Splendored Thing.*
5. c. *As the World Turns.*

Q Quiz #2: Soap Towns

1. d. An earthquake and a subsequent killer wave struck the town of Sunset Beach, California on NBC's *Sunset Beach* in the summer of 1998. In an eerie coincidence, the fictional "Shock Wave" disaster aired on the same day a *real*

tsunami devastated Papua, New Guinea. "We were appalled to read about the earthquake and tsunami that occurred in New Guinea," the soap's producer, Aaron Spelling, stated in a press release at the time. "On *Sunset Beach*, we had also staged an earthquake and tidal wave. Our shooting of these episodes occurred weeks before the New Guinea catastrophe. We sincerely hope that our fans and the press realize that. Had we known beforehand of the impending disaster in New Guinea, we would never have created a similar story line." In the summer of 2005, NBC's politically incorrect *Passions* unleashed a tsunami on the town of Harmony; this was rather uncomfortably soon after real-life tsunamis had devastated Southeast Asia earlier that year.

2. a. *One Life to Live*. Back in 1989, the underground city of Eterna was discovered to be buried deep within the Llantano Mountains outside of Llanview, Pennsylvania.

3. b. *Full Circle*. In the early '60s, Dyan Cannon played Lisa Crowder, the heroine of this short-lived NBC sudser about a young Virginian widow.

4. c. *Loving* was set in the East Coast town of Corinth. Later, the show changed its name to *The City* and moved to New York City's Soho neighborhood.

5. d. *The Clear Horizon*.

Q Quiz #3: Soap Families

1. d. The Bauers.
2. b. Powdered doughnuts.
3. c. The Spencers. Back in 1993, Luke, Laura, and Lucky Spencer operated the Triple L Diner in Canada while hiding out from mobster Frank Smith.
4. d. Christian Slater played the non-Ryan role of D. J. Lasalle back in 1985.
5. a. Victor Newman has four living, biological kids: Victoria, Nicholas, Victor Jr., and Abby.

Q Quiz #4: Soap Hunks

1. c. The ab-licious Alec Musser won the *All My Children* contract role of Del Hunkle as the Season 2 winner of SOAPnet's *I Wanna Be a Soap Star*.
2. b. Christopher Durham stayed shirtless during the entire summer of '82, as *Capitol* lifeguard Matt McCandless.
3. a. Doug Davidson. Although two-time *Playgirl* poser Diamont bared his derriere during a special 1995 primetime episode of *The Young and the Restless*, Davidson did it during a daytime episode first!
4. d. Maurice Benard—who was born Mauricio Jose Morales—has played Mafia heartthrob Michael "Sonny" Corinthos on *General Hospital* since 1993.

5. d. Josh Duhamel definitely posed *au naturel* in his early career, but not in *Playgirl*.

Q Quiz # 5: Soap Divas

1. e. Joan Allen has never appeared on a daytime soap. Joan Crawford filled in for her ailing daughter, Christina Crawford, on *The Secret Storm* in 1968. Christina famously bitched about her has-been mama's audacity in her book, *Mommie Dearest*. *Dynasty* diva Joan Collins did a six-month stint as Alexandra Spaulding on *Guiding Light* in 2002. *Knots Landing* star Joan Van Ark played trailer-trash socialite Gloria Fisher Abbott on *The Young and the Restless* from 2004-05. Van Ark also played Janie Whitney on *Days of our Lives* back in 1970. Old Hollywood screen siren Joan Fontaine scored a Daytime Emmy nomination for playing Paige Williams on *Ryan's Hope* in 1980.

2. b. Robin Strasser has played *One Life to Live*'s Dorian Lord on and off since 1979.

3. c. Genie Francis has played three soap characters on four shows. In addition to her most famous role as *General Hospital*'s Laura Vining Webber Baldwin Spencer, Francis was *Days of our Lives*'s Diana Colville and *All My Children*'s Ceara Connor Hunter, who later appeared on Loving. Francis also starred in the primetime sudser *Bare Essence* as Tyger Hayes.

4. e. Morgan Fairchild. a. Erika Slezak has won six Daytime Emmy Awards for outstanding lead actress.

Q Quiz #6: Soap Gender Benders

1. c. Carlotta Chang played a male-to-female transgender woman named Azure C. on ABC's *The City* from 1995-96.

2. b. Shady underworld figure RJ Gannon (Timothy D. Stickney) hired drag queen Wendi Mercury to bartend at his club, Capricorn, in 1997. Performance artist Gary Hall, also known as Shequida, played Wendi.

3. d. When *Days of our Lives* star Alison Sweeney went on maternity leave in 2005, her Sami character masqueraded as a man named Stan, who was played by Dan Wells. He had previously been a straight contestant on Bravo's gay-themed reality TV dating show, *Boy Meets Boy* in 2003.

4. b. Krystal Lake.

5. b. In *Soapdish*'s hilarious climax, it was revealed that Montana Moorehead—the blonde, bossy *The Sun Also Sets* star played by Cathy Moriarity—was born Milton Moorehead.

ACKNOWLEDGMENTS

AS A SENIOR EDITOR at TVGuide.com, I write about soap operas for a living, and have had the privilege of interviewing many of the actors, industry insiders, publicists, and other folks who make up the world of television daytime drama for my job. And while I did have previous quotes and stories from past interviews to help flesh out this book, the vast majority of the quotes in *The Q Guide to Soap Operas* are the result of brand-new interviews, conducted especially for this book.

My thanks to the many daytime TV stars who graciously took the time to participate in this project, whether they gave me a minute on the red carpet or sat down for an hour-long dishfest. These well-known luminaries included (in alphabetical order) Thom Bierdz, Tanya Boyd, Jeff Branson, Kathy Brier, Darlene Conley, Jeanne Cooper, Michael Corbett, Linda Dano, Anthony Geary, Elizabeth Hubbard, Finola Hughes, Katherine Kelly Lang, Juliet Mills, Joshua Morrow, Lara Parker, Austin Peck, Colleen Zenk Pinter, Eden Riegel, Lisa Rinna, Emma Samms, Kristoff St. John, Robin Strasser, Alison Sweeney, Gordon Thomson, Heather Tom, Helen Wagner, and Tuc Watkins.

I also appreciated fabulously bright insights and

stories from sassy interviewees like Michael Bruno, Charles Busch, Thom Racina, Mimi Torchin, and a few gracious gay Hollywood personalities who have asked that they not be named for career reasons.

Additional courtesies were extended by PR professionals, including Michael Cohen, Lauri Hogan, Mitchell Messinger, and Abbie Schiller of ABC Daytime; *B&B*'s Eva Demirjian and Jennifer Mulhall; BWR's Carrie Simons; Andrea McKinnon of Corday Productions; Gina Anderson and Wendy Luckenbill of NBC Daytime; Scott Barton of *Passions*; PMK's Meghan Prophet; Cristin Callaghan and Alan Locher of Procter and Gamble; SOAPnet's Jori Petersen and Penni Ellington; *Y&R*'s Elise Bromberg and Julie Mitchell; Thomas DeLorenzo; Brenda Feldman; Steve Rohr; Charles Sherman; and Vivien Stern.

Special thanks to the famed celebrity biographer J. Randy Taraborrelli for his friendship and professional mentorship.

I am appreciative to my boss, TVGuide.com's Director of Content, Daniel Manu, for his encouragement of my foray into first-time authorship and my career in general.

I am also appreciative to the editors of my alma mater, *Soaps In Depth* magazine, Dawn Mazzurco, Charlie Mason, and Richard Simms, for giving me a great start in entertainment journalism. Working at *SID* was truly like going to soap-opera grad school! Thanks especially to Richard for reading my *Q Guide* manuscript with a second pair of expert eyes.

Major props must go to Joseph Pittman, my editor at Alyson Books and a loyal TVGuide.com reader, who paid me the highest compliment possible by offering me the opportunity to write this book.

Also, hugs all around to my special friends who have supported this sudsy effort in ways tangible and intangible, including Dr. Alexander P.W. Hughes, Bill Givens, Dave Anderson, Dianne Faucher, Jeffrey Epstein, Damian J. Holbrook, Troy Douglas Mendez, and Kiyomi Mizukami.

The biggest thanks of all go to my Italian-American mama, Maria Bond, to whom this book is dedicated because she always believed in me.

BIBLIOGRAPHY

Christina Crawford. *Mommie Dearest*. New York: Morrow, 1978.

Tab Hunter with Eddie Muller. *Tab Hunter Confidential*. New York: Algonquin Books of Chapel Hill, 2005.

Robert LaGuardia. *Soap World*. New York: Arbor House Publishing Company, 1983.

Julie Poll. *Another World: The 35th Anniversary Celebration*. New York: HarperCollins Publishers, 1999.

Christopher Schemering. *The Soap Opera Encyclopedia*. New York: Ballantine, 1987.

Gary Warner. *All My Children Complete Family Scrapbook*. Santa Monica, CA: General Publishing Group, 1994.

Gary Warner. *One Life to Live: Thirty Years of Memories*. New York: Hyperion, 1998.